Out on a

Growing Up
on One Leg

by
Harry Wade

Happy Birthday
Roy

Best wishes
Harry Wade

One-Legged Publications

First published in Great Britain in 2009 by One-Legged Publications

ISBN 978-0-9564062-0-0

Printed and bound in Great Britain by CPI Antony Rowe, Eastbourne, UK

Acknowledgements

My thanks to Mary for helping me to start writing this in the first place and to my father Christopher for helping to bring it to its published state; also my thanks for encouragement and suggestions from my sister Joanna, Hugh and Kristine Black-Hawkins, Rowan Lawton, Andy Hopkinson, Janet Browning, Ellie Munro, Tricia Jessiman, Fran Farrar, Bill Badham, Jake Manning and especially to Jim Preston for his help with the design.

*To Mary, Matthew, Robert and Katherine
and to my father, my sister and my mother*

CONTENTS

1963. The small red trike with yellow wheels hurtled down the steep hill. The little boy's feet were no longer on the pedals fixed to the front wheel. The boy's mother began to run but she was too far behind to reach him. The pedals flailed menacingly as the trike reached terminal velocity and the junction at the bottom of the hill loomed. The boy heard his mother cry out with increasing anxiety – much to his satisfaction. As he whizzed past the last house but one, he jammed his metal leg into the pedals and they froze. The trike slewed to a halt leaving a very pleasing skid mark down a series of paving stones. He turned and grinned at his mother who was just arriving out of breath: "That was fun! Can we do it again?" "Perhaps tomorrow", she winced.

INTRODUCTION

My unique selling point is my leg; the artificial one. In this book, I reveal quite a lot of my one leg: how I was 'born like it', learned to walk on it and later faced the quandary of whether to take it off secretly when trying to get into bed with a girl.

But *what kind of man am I?* How have my disabilities affected me as I grew up? I have tried to look behind 'the man in the iron leg' and explain a bit more about the range of things that have made me who I am and not just who made my legs. I am more sensitive about the two fingers missing from my right hand, although less spectacular or memorable for other people than my leg, as they are always in the public gaze, while the artificial leg is mostly hidden down the trousers.

I've mostly kept my thoughts hidden inside too even though my artificial leg has never kept me indoors. My feelings about it have ebbed and flowed, both positive and negative, but one way or another I have always been out on a limb.

Aged 4 on my trike, with metal knee hinges just poking through

2

"BORN LIKE IT"

I'M ALWAYS ASKED: "How did it happen?" I'm not sure whether people expect or even hope for some gory tale of carnage and trauma. I have told an awestruck audience a tragic tale of bull-running in Pamplona, where the missing leg would acquire trophy status. But actually I was just born like it.

In July 1959, at Queen Mary's Nursing Home in Hampstead, North London, I was born with a 'club' right foot and fingers missing on the right hand. Club means deformed or simply 'not a proper shape'. My right thumb was fully functional but the two remaining fingers were webbed together. I also had a 'hammer' thumb on my left hand, which meant that it was stuck at a right angle. Unexpected before and unexplained since, I have never been able to be sure of the cause of the birth defect.

I am a year or two too old for Thalidomide, which was mainly in the early 1960s. There was a lingering suspicion over something my great aunt, who had been a nurse, gave my mother once for her morning sickness, although this was never proven. Early on I was told that I may have been lying on the hand and leg in the womb, which seems unlikely. A consultant recently told me that my disability was probably "just one of those things".

There is a suggestion of a cause in the book *Mutants* by Armand Marie Leroi. This describes how because of "Hox genes" the body's cells either divide or fail to divide at crucial times in the womb. Unexpected mutation can result in a baby having a range of malformations of limbs. The author describes one condition that matches very closely my own:

> *"A particularly devastating mutation that deletes no fewer than nine Hox genes in one go causes infants to be born with missing bones in the forearm, missing fingers and missing toes."*

He goes on to say that this mutation sometimes also affects the penis, although he doesn't say that it necessarily makes it smaller.

It hadn't occurred to me that my parents would have been distressed when I was born with a disability. I felt so loved as a child that the disadvantage factor never came through. Many years later a friend of my father mentioned to me in passing how upset my dad was at the time. I suppose it's obvious really. A recent magazine article about dads of babies born with a disability talks of their sense of grief, loss and anger; so, if this did apply in my case, my parents certainly hid it or got over it well. My parents spent a lot of time after my birth seeking advice as to the possible causes and the likely legacy. It was a very tense time running up to the birth of my own children, not knowing what sort of legacy might be passed on to them.

My mother kept a 'Baby Book' both for my older sister, Joanna, and for me. Joanna, by the way, was born officially 'completely normal'. She actually had a slightly wonky eye as a little girl and I tagged along when she visited a friendly specialist to play exciting games of 'spot the yellow birdie' out of the corner of her lazy eye. But my impairments were bigger and better...

My Baby Book catalogue of illnesses reads: 25th Feb-2nd March 1960 – Cold; 6th-10th June – Fever & rash; 17th June – Leg operation in Great Ormond Street. The list continues and, before we get to measles, mumps and chicken pox, it includes 4th May 1961 – Hammer thumb released on left hand; and 20th March 1962 right hand operated on in University College Hospital under the friendly consultant Mr D.N. Matthews. This hand operation separated the webbing joining my existing two fingers, with skin taken from my thigh to patch. So my childhood health record had a mix of the mundane and the exotic. I spent several days in hospital sharing a room with my mother. The games we played included whose raindrop would get to the bottom of the window first? and who would spot the next Number 73 big red bus?

Mother and baby doing well

I was not quite one year old for the leg operation in 1960. The bill from Great Ormond Street totalled £70 and 16 shillings, but my parents were determined to seek the best possible help. This was for a Symes operation, named after the surgeon who invented it. Readers of a sensitive disposition may wish to look away now. It features the 'disarticulation' of the foot at the ankle, which means the amputation of the limb through a joint without the cutting of bone. They remove the knobbly ankle bits and use the heel flap to cover the end of the stump. The combination of not cutting the bone and having the heel flap as unbroken skin means that the stump can be reasonably load-bearing. I developed a loping style of crawling and a particularly vigorous way of climbing stairs using the stump as a grappling hook.

Early pictures from The Baby Book

And then I learned to walk with my first artificial leg. The Baby Book records that I stood up in June 1960, the same month as my operation, and stood up alone in November that year; I took my first steps without help on 10th December, aged 1½.

I was living my new life and at the time blissfully unaware of what impact I was having around me. I have already mentioned my teenage discovery of my parents' reaction to my disability. In another chapter I've looked at an even later discovery I made about how Joanna met my arrival, and it turned out not to be all smiles for the cute and cuddly baby brother.

My learning to walk attracted the attention of our family's home movies, which were on hand to record my very early attempts with the new metal leg. My bottle green dungarees glowed as my faltering steps were supported on either side by my mother and by home help Mrs Sandy. Unscripted, across the camera came big sister Joanna. She was sporting her grandmother's white gloves and fox fur (the fur now, of course, renounced). She stared purposefully into the lens, briefly adopted a very exaggerated limb-dragging limp and then sprinted off. Watch this space!

But it was too late to run rings round me forever. The final bulletin from the Baby Book reports that I too was "running around freely" in April 1961. I was on the grid. I had the technology and I was up, up and away – nothing could stop me now.

Trouble Afoot

So what was the one-legged 'toddler about town' wearing in the 1960s? The earliest model of leg I had consisted of a wooden foot, metal casing, leather socket, metal hinges and leather-buckled thigh corset. As I was relatively unrestrained in thought and deed, these would respectively break, dent, split, bow and snap. It was never wilful damage, it was just how I lived a normal, active childhood. The buckles and straps on the thigh corset were eventually replaced by Velcro straps, which made taking it on and off a bit easier, but the essential technology of the artificial leg remained very similar for the first twenty years of my life.

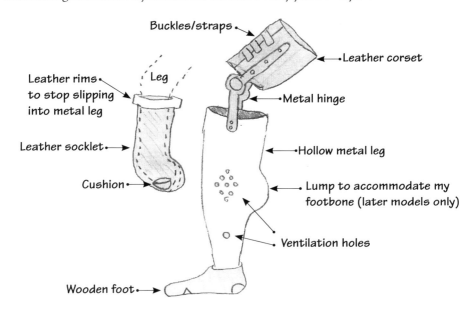

The leather socket in which my 'real' leg sat was moulded in the shape of my stump with a little cushion at the bottom. This is similar to an ordinary foot inside a shoe and I wore a silky nylon inner sock and a thicker woollen outer sock. This served to cushion the leg against the hard surfaces, protect against rubbing and deal with the perspiration. As with any shoe, there is movement of the foot inside the casing and, if it is the wrong shape in any place, there is a danger of blisters. The socks, particularly when sweaty, could get wrinkled and create pressure points, and the woollen ones did tend to get harder and matted when washed so frequently. On a bad day I'd get very painful blisters, which would only heal by leaving my leg off. But not wearing the leg meant hopping or sitting down and mostly I would rather have the discomfort than the disability.

The socket then fitted into the hollow casing of the 'metal leg'. This is what I always called it, although the professionals call it an artificial limb or prosthesis. The metal legs were a fairly standard shape, made to a series of standard lengths. Eventually I required a non-standard shaped metal casing as my stump grew at a different angle, but more of that below.

The leather thigh corset, connected to the metal leg by two big hinges, served two purposes of taking some of my weight off the stump as I stepped on it and then helping to grip and to pick up the metal leg as I stepped off it. The knee hinges also helped to keep my leg straight as I walked, by keeping my foot pointing forwards at all times. They did look particularly odd, thrusting out of my trousers on either side of my knee, and they were a serious cause of trouser-erosion, especially when crawling or playing on the floor.

The early feet were really useless. My first feet were made as two pieces of wood joined flexibly (and fallibly) by a piece of woven material. With no ankle mechanism the foot took a real bashing from the rocking movement of walking, running, kicking and slamming my foot into the flailing pedals of my bike. The flimsy piece of material that joined the toe-bit-of-wood to the foot-bit-of-wood had no chance of keeping up and I constantly had a floppy front-of-foot that made me pitch forward too easily for an elegant catwalk strut. But I cannot say that this seriously hindered me during this time, and the floppy-toed right foot was a long way from the centre of the important things in life for a boy growing up. You adapt.

All my legs have been provided by The National Health Service and I have been exceptionally lucky to have had a series of care professionals who invested their skills, and later their devolved budgets, to give me the best possible quality of life. The 'fitters' are the wizards and artists that measure, mould and fit the legs. Jack Cosnett fitted my first ever leg at Roehampton Limb Fitting Centre and continued to do so over the next 20 years. This consistent quality of knowledge and care from Jack was a huge help in getting and keeping me mobile. He was exceptionally skilled and way ahead of his time in involving me closely in the process of getting the legs as right for me as possible. Today the preferred 'social model of disability' starts with the person and looks how society can help to integrate them; in the 1960s the widespread 'medical model' dictated that the doctors are experts and they will decide what is best for the disabled patient.

I had a new leg every nine months as I was growing up. You may imagine the difficulty of keeping comfortable and wearable a leg that needed such precision fitting when my body was changing shape so rapidly. My mother and I visited Roehampton on a three-monthly basis for the cycle of measuring, fitting and collection. This involved a lengthy round-trip across London from Hampstead where we lived. Before my mother learned to drive, my father often dropped us off on the way to work in Shepherd's Bush. The return journey featured a 72 bus to Barnes, a train to Waterloo and a tube home. Occasionally people stopped to offer lifts to a young mother and child at the bus stop – a sociable sign of the times – but otherwise it was public transport all the way. Another sign of the times was that we struck up a relationship with the ticket inspector at Chalk Farm tube station. It became a tradition that we broke our tube journey here to call in at Marine Ices. I always had mango sorbet and Mother always had nut crunch. We had a 'friendly chat' with Mrs Manzi at Marine Ices and then another 'friendly chat' with the ticket inspector who would let us back on the tube without having to buy another ticket. I really loved these cosy, companionable days.

My mother was truly wonderful at 'friendly chats'. I hope to have inherited even a small fraction of her amazing ability to engage with complete strangers and to make the meeting feel positive. I must have learned some of the rules of engagement on these long days out with my mother. I do remember them as happy days and it was certainly 'quality time' that we spent together. It is interesting to reflect that it was my disability that was buying or qualifying me for this time, as it always felt like a treat when I was a boy – and not just a day out of school. I remember playing endless Battleships, and other games that we took with us, in between yet more friendly chats with Renee at the reception desk in Roehampton and with the woman at the hospital café, where we always had tinned salmon sandwiches on white bread.

In contrast I got a real earful once from a hospital porter for crashing a wheelchair while racing Joanna, who was on a rare visit with us. Most of all I got a terrible telling-off from Dr J_____ for wasting NHS resources in getting my leg wet by sitting under a fund-raising ducking stool at a school fete. It's true that water and metal legs do not mix, although it soon dried off in the sun like the rest of me. Dr J_____ and Dr V_____ were two of a number of doctors that I saw at Roehampton. While Jack the Fitter was a wizard, most of the doctors were trolls. Jack knew the curves of my leg intimately and was dedicated to making me as mobile as possible, while the doctors always seemed to be slumped in their private gloomy cave in another part of the building. They were, at best, indifferent to how I lived my active life and, at times, disapproving. What a contrast then to the mission statement of Otto Bock, one of today's limb suppliers: "The purpose of our corporate activities is to improve the quality of life for people with limited mobility". The original working title of this book was "When Dr J_____ wasn't looking", because it felt like the most active and exciting bits of my childhood were smuggled out behind his back. As far as Jack was concerned, he wanted me to be as adventurous as possible, even though he had to pick up the pieces – literally, in some cases.

With the notable exception of Dr Puddyfoot (vocational perhaps?) many of the doctors were decommissioned or pensioned off military men and in my experience their attitude was generally deeply negative. I always had to see a doctor to sign off the latest leg but this usually only meant the briefest of exchanges. They were hardly ever seen in the fitting rooms, but carried the professional clout that attracted more deference from Jack than I could explain from personal experience. It may have been a military or class thing, as Jack was a decent, old-fashioned man who respected figures of authority and he was the right age to have served in the war. The medical model of disability was totally dominant and most people in those days would have been used to obeying the authority of a doctor without question.

The danger of this is when the doctor declares: "you have an artificial leg... you are disabled... you cannot ride a bike... and you cannot climb ladders". This sentence was not said to or passed on me, but it was said to another boy I met at Roehampton with an identical disability. This other boy attended a special school and believed that he could not ride a bike or climb ladders, while I'd been crashing my bike and falling off five-bar gates for years by that time.

The early home movie film also shows me walking rather knock-kneed but not discomfited by wearing the artificial leg. I'm seen running up and down sand dunes in a rather ungainly but serviceable way. If you haven't got an ankle, it is so crucial to have the knee for a smooth walk (and later for braking and accelerating in a car and for getting any sensitivity into the little half-volley drop shots at tennis). People with an above-knee amputation usually have a more visible, rolling gait where they have to wait for the leg to swing forward and lock before they can put their weight on it again.

I loved the red trike that I first described in the introduction. In May and June of 1962, aged nearly 3, my baby book records that I first learned to ride the trike, control my pedal car, climb ladders and five-bar gates and "play football vigorously". It was typical of my parents to encourage and enable rather than restrain me.

I have a disability, but in many ways I know I have been lucky, perhaps privileged. I think it is better to be born with it rather than have to adjust to it in later life; I have no sense of loss or bitterness and relatively few phantom pains in the toes that aren't there. I was born and grew up in Hampstead, which was more bohemian than bling in the 1960s, more writers and artists than footballers and pop stars, so socialist and civilised. We were relatively well off, meaning we could afford the £70 and 16 shillings for my first operation and we could afford to employ Mrs Sandy as 'mother's help' to clean, babysit and catch me when I fell. There were no other children with one leg at my schools, but the liberal and tolerant neighbourhood must have contributed to the absence of bullying that I can recall. My needs were never deemed 'special' enough to consider sending me to a 'special' school. My mother patched and re-patched my corduroy trousers, but ultimately we could afford to replace them and the shoes I battered and the socks I destroyed in the extra wear and tear of an active artificial leg-wearer.

Most of all, I am lucky to have grown up with positive attitude in and around me. My father, now widowed for over 15 years, recently said how grateful he was to have inherited his positive thinking from his mother. My parents both showed me an unswervingly positive approach to life. Ability and disability are sometimes governed by a frame of mind – of yourself and also of your loved ones.

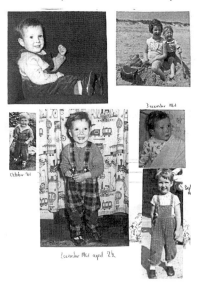

Dungaree-orama: toddler pictures from The Baby Book

FAMILY MATTERS

My christening in All Hallows, Upper Dean. Bedfordshire
Left to right: sister Joanna, mother Diana, grandmother Eileen, father Christopher, great aunt Nancy, grandfather Taid

AS A TODDLER, the most important person in my life was: me, of course, like any other toddler. I had a close bond with my mother, as I have described; she called me 'Foglamp' or 'Triffic' or a vast range of other spontaneous terms of endearment that were mostly made up on the spot and didn't mean anything very much, other than she loved me. You can ask my children what this feels like as I seem to have inherited it too.

My relationship with my dad is now excellent, although fathers in the 1950s and 60s were not supposed to have a hands-on role in child-rearing. Dad was persuaded to go to work on the day I was born and Mum was already sitting up eating liver and bacon for lunch when he arrived hotfoot from Shepherd's Bush. Joanna and I were bathed and in our pyjamas ready for when he got home from work, so weekday times with Dad mainly consisted of a hug from the lower portions of his suit. It was a treat when he would make up bedtime stories for us – mine were often about a dog called Bonzo and his mates – and we had a special treat at the end of the week with the 'Friday Night Presents'. Dad would herald his return home from work and the start of the family weekend with a small gift he had picked up along the way. One week I got the coveted furry Esso tiger's tail and the 1970 World Cup Coins kept me going for months. At the weekend, Dad would play tennis and Joanna and I would participate in the post-match bath when he came home. This involved him pretending that his feet were seals, including authentic animal noises, and we would try to put our plastic tooth mugs on them as they surfaced from the soapy water. It was a popular game that we played for a long time. I can still feel the cold, hard side of the bath pressing on my chest as I hung there with both hands clutching the plastic beakers.

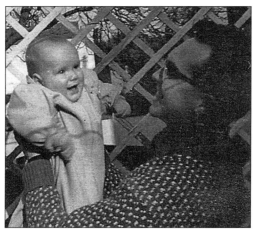

Father and baby doing well too

Dad tried unsuccessfully to share my interest in football. He took me to my first English game, Arsenal v Everton, which was odd for a budding Chelsea fan. Later he did take me to see the Blues, when we sat in the previous 'new, posh' West Stand before the current one. There still wasn't much atmosphere and I should have been more grateful for Dad piping up with "Come on Ossie" (rhyming with glossy), but I was cross with him for mispronouncing the name of the King of Stamford Bridge. I do appreciate more now his efforts to link with me in my 'difficult teenage years' (although of course I have no memory of being difficult, ever).

My mum and dad were very close, with never a cross word in my hearing. Mum seemed to be the emotional link to us for a man who had had so much expression beaten out of him in his own childhood. I learned later how he had been his mother's golden boy and he wanted only to sing with his golden voice. But he was overshadowed by his eldest brother, constrained by his sickly other brother, never allowed to speak at meals and miserably incarcerated at public school. It was hard for him when we were young to get close, and not really considered to be 'his job'.

On holidays we would be delighted to see much more of him in a relaxed and playful mood, including his romantic side as he sang "The silvery moon upon the lagoon" to my mother. After we went to a bullfight in Spain, we reconstructed it back at the house. Joanna was the bullfighter, I was the crazy nutter that ran around to distract the bull if things went wrong, Dad was the wild snorting bull and Mum was the sexy cow they brought in at the end to calm the bull down and get him safely out of the ring. Aged 10, it felt good to see my gentle dad as a wild snorting bull but a bit weird to see my mum as a sexy cow.

I spent all of my childhood at home with my sister, of course. We were born 21 months apart, but we never attended the same school or had any friends in common. Joanna went to a different nursery school and then South Hampstead High School for Girls (only).

My sister Jaj (Joanna) leading from the front as usual

We had some fun and adventures together, mostly at weekends and holidays, again as described elsewhere. I think we are both quite competitive, as so many siblings are, and this contributed to a pattern of family life over the years. Joanna from an early stage declined to play family card or board games. At the time I thought she was just a spoilsport, but her later explanation was that she detected my parents deliberately trying to let me win (as one does sometimes to encourage a hapless beginner). The injustice of this rigged, guaranteed no-win situation prompted her to opt out and do her homework instead. "What's the point of competing if you know you are not going to win anyway?" I need to say, here and now, that I am not claiming any credit whatsoever for the fact that Joanna's diligent stints of homework led her to achieve magnificent academic results. She was part of a fiercely competitive bunch of girls at school and got excellent grades in her 'O' levels and 'A' levels and an 'Exhibition' to Cambridge University. My own version of "What's the point of competing if you know you are not going to win anyway?" certainly affected me as I meandered, under-prepared up to my exams, always that one year behind Joanna's most recent triumph. Well I wasn't going to get straight A grades was I, so what was the point in trying? I've never been able to channel my competitive streak into academic pursuits. Joanna was rubbish at driving when she first started and I held a strong hope that I might actually pass my test before her, but the 21 months head-start proved long enough, she passed first time and I was left with the scant consolation prize of having had fewer lessons. Does this count as a sibling complex or just normal rivalry? I comforted myself by thinking that I was relatively 'more qualified in the school of life' and I nonchalantly agreed to take Joanna to her first disco and to *Cabaret*, her first X-film, so there.

I spent a fair bit of my childhood with Mrs Sandy too. Mrs Sandy (short for Sanderburg) was a broad bespectacled woman who was never seen without her blue nylon housecoat. She was kind and loving and went pink and wheezy when she laughed a lot. She was a harder disciplinarian than my mother, but she did let us stay up to watch *Coronation Street* and we were surprised to discover that there was a third channel called ITV. My dad worked for The BBC and it was mostly frowned upon to watch 'the other side', let alone soap operas like *Corro*. I must point out that, many years later, mum and dad developed a guilty secret habit of watching *Dallas*, but at least that was on The BBC.

Mrs Sandy had a motor scooter. She rigged up a piece of hardboard that served as a back seat and would take us for a ride round the block. It involved the same steep hill as the trike story and was similarly hair-raising for all concerned – apart from Mrs Sandy who was driving. I'm sure my mum couldn't watch as we went weaving off down the same hill. I tried to get my short arms around as much of Mrs Sandy's waist as possible – nearly half way possibly – and tucked my thumbs into the belt loops as the grip on the nylon housecoat was negligible.

Testing the throttle on Mrs Sandy's scooter, watched by Joanna and Hamish the builder

We called my mother's father Taid. He was born into a large family in Liverpool and sent as a boy to live with cousins in Amlwch in Anglesey. A tailor by trade, he went on to become mayor of the town and fiercely and proudly Welsh. Taid was proper-job working class and a very good man. I was barely 11 when he died, so I mostly have just childhood memories of him. I remember him as tall with lots of white hair – he was balding on top, but with a certain amount coming out of his ears and nose. I remember him dressed quite formally, always wearing collar and cuffs, perhaps as a tailor should. He wore grey flannel trousers, even on the beach. Most of all he was jovial and funny. We had a much-loved routine for his Christmas stocking. Instead of the chocolates and tangerines, his stocking would contain a lump of coal and a piece of brick, wrapped in newspaper. We would shriek with laughter as he unwrapped each item and exclaim how happy he was to get it and what fun he would have with it. Taid always packed his stocking himself, although early on we assumed it was Father Christmas with a sense of humour, and Taid introduced it as part of the Christmas fun and games.

Taid had served in the Navy in the Great War and his ship was torpedoed. This trauma (or adventure) did not register with me as a child to anything like the same extent as the fact that, in the navy, he had learned to peel apples in one long curly snake. Taid would do his grandfatherly duty by taking Joanna and me out for a walk on Hampstead Heath. We would sit on a bench on Parliament Hill and he would get out his penknife and create the green serpent before our eyes. The apple always tasted extra special when the preparation had been so appealing and the skin was the best bit. Taid had also learned to box in the navy. He may have shown me a few moves, or just been trying to fend me off as a bouncing boy, but I learned his best catchphrase: "I'm going to bash him on the boko" (i.e. punch him on the nose).

In my Christening gown with Taid, my grandfather, John Bennett Hughes

We visited him in Anglesey most years, when we would usually stay in a house down the road from Amlwch, near Lligwy beach. On the beach, with his grey flannel trousers rolled up, Taid would lead the stream-damming, the sandcastle-cum-ball-run and he taught me how to skim stones and make a catapult. Taid has the distinction of taking me, and Joanna, to our first ever live football match: the mighty Blues... of Bangor City. The most memorable bit of the match was when the big defender hoofed the ball into Row G, the very back of the tiny stand of brightly painted benches. It bashed a female spectator on the boko, as we appreciated, and many of the players trooped over to commiserate in person.

Taid's terraced house in Amlwch felt small when we went for tea, and he still had a working outside loo, but there was nothing negative about his modest house or his Welshness as far as we were concerned. Mum, I later learned, was rather self-conscious about her origins and Dad was discouraged from learning the language, even though he did it with respect. Nevertheless Joanna and I learned some key words, partly from a set of paper napkins that had cartoons of things with their Welsh names. Mum often cooked stwnch fa for lunch, a delicious mix of mashed broad beans with buttermilk and crispy bacon. Dad still keeps his coats in the twll tan grisiau, the cupboard under the stairs, *pwmpan* sounds a much politer word for breaking wind and I can still hear my mother exclaim *"Achavee!"* when I'd stood in something particularly nasty, though she may have made this up. Pronouncing the full version of *Llanfairpwlchgwnygyllgogerachwnydrobwllchllandisilliogogogoch*, the longest railway station name in the UK, was childsplay.

Eileen Wade was my father's mother and the only other of my grandparents that I met. She was known as 'The Queen of Dean'. This is because of her extensive power and influence; mostly through sheer force of character and partly because she used to live in The Big House (and employed people) before it was commandeered and trashed during the war. Granny moved into more modest premises of Bryant Cottage, without the employees, in the same village of Upper Dean. She still ran the Women's Legion, was president of the annual Flower Show committee and chairman of the village school's board of governors. The current school in Dean that all my children attended, is named after their great grandmother and, with a high tide mark of 46 pupils, is hanging on resolutely to survival. This is very appropriate for a woman who was totally resolute and thoroughly great, including physical dimensions.

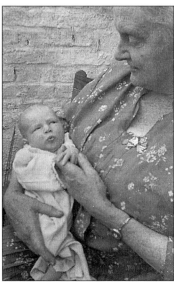

Exchanging mutually suspicious looks with my grandmother, Eileen Wade

The family went to Dean, about 60 miles north of London, every other weekend. Granny was from the old school of 'children should be seen and not heard' and mealtimes were a particular trial. Saying grace and table manners were top of the agenda. As soon as my elbow got anywhere near the tabletop Granny would remark: "All joints on the table shall be carved" and her set jaw would show that this was partly funny and mostly a criticism. She had a legendary constitution and, despite wobbly dentures, I witnessed her chomping her way through an entire artichoke including the thistly bits you are supposed to remove. Another time she baked a summer fruit pie and set it to cool on the windowsill with the old pastry funnel in the middle. A small swarm of wasps, attracted by the sweet fruit, flew down the funnel and perished in the boiling filling. On serving, the wasps were discovered and the rest of us politely pushed them to one side of the plate – but Granny just carried on chomping.

Towards the end of her life, Granny's mobility deteriorated. She drove, eccentrically, until a crash forced her to take her first ever test (hadn't needed them when she started). After a few blocks the examiner asked her to pull in at the side of the road. He opened his door and said: "Mrs Wade, I am walking back to the test centre where I will arrange for someone to collect you, it is too dangerous to continue: you have failed!" Despite this she acquired a rather exciting motorised 3-wheeled invalid carriage. Like the modern versions – also lethal, in my opinion – it did not require a driving licence and had a top speed of 12 miles an hour in which she could tour the village. Although Joanna and I enjoyed driving it down the short drive (if at full speed you slammed it into reverse it had a nostalgic skid just like my old trike) Granny smashed too many gateposts and ran over too many pets – mostly her own, thankfully – to be worthwhile.

She went from a walking frame to a wheelchair and began to occupy downstairs rooms, including when she came to stay for Christmas. Now I know I shouldn't be unsympathetic to someone with a disability... but as a 13 year-old I thoroughly resented that what I considered to be the TV lounge with the piano in became Granny's bedroom and out of bounds. And my joints were threatened with carving in my own house. Granny's determination meant that we still all went to the theatre long before disabled access was a consideration. The London Coliseum won the prize as the flattest access, as long as you sat in a box rather than the normal seats. There was only one set of steps where we needed rent-a-shot-putter to get Granny and her chair up to the next level and getting her to the ladies loo at the interval meant some strategic scouting and barricading to permit the male strong-arm support at key moments.

Unlike with Taid, I didn't really bond with Granny. She died in 1973, when I was just 14, before we could reach any mutual understanding or appreciation. She didn't do children and I didn't do Victorians. Dad was the youngest of her three sons. Michael, the middle son, died of a prolonged degenerative disease aged 17; and Dad remembers not being allowed to shriek for years, in case it disturbed the sick sibling. The eldest son turned out to be Professor Sir William Wade, or 'Hank' as his students at Caius College Cambridge knew him. Uncle Bill, as I knew him, single-handedly held the British Government to account through constitutional law, drafted the national constitution for Uganda and, most excitingly, once ran me round his garden in a wheelbarrow. Once being the operative word here, as the word 'ascetic' might have been invented for him. We saw very little of Uncle Bill when I was growing up and I found his dry, intellectual image rather scary. He was not nearly as scary, though, as his first wife Marie, from whom I always felt great waves of disapproval, regardless of what I was doing. Her greatest palpable hit on me was to write to my parents to complain that I appeared tipsy standing in the fountain at their son's wedding. I had drunk champagne, given to me by their daughter-in-law, but I was only *pretending* to be drunk and there were several other people in the fountain before me, your worship. But there was nothing scary about Marjorie, Uncle Bill's second wife, for whom the word 'glam' didn't do her justice. She rejuvenated Uncle Bill, I once saw him without a tie on, and she turned up to my wedding in a radiant turquoise outfit. This was offset by a radiant turquoise chiffon scarf, but she sidled up to my mother and declared: "My dear, not many people would realise that this, round my neck, is actually a pair of tights". Good on yer, Marjorie!

SCHOOL DAYS

MY FIRST SCHOOL, in May 1963, was Mrs Meyer's Nursery School in Kemplay Road in Hampstead. The big steps led up to the door of the towering Victorian terraced building, so typical of the grand local architecture. Inside there was a dark hallway where we hung our coats – my peg had a picture of an aeroplane on it – and a big light room where we spent our mornings. I fondly recall jumping off the climbing frames, making pretty patterns with shiny shapes and threading beads.

For exercise we walked in a crocodile down to the children's enclosure on nearby Hampstead Heath. There were no facilities there then other than a sandpit. So we charged around playing tag and maybe a bit of football. For some reason I was allowed one day to wear to school my father's war medals pinned to my jumper. They jingled attractively and had very pretty coloured ribbons. At the end of the day it was discovered that I had one medal less. We returned to the playground to comb the slopes and sandpit, but we never found it. I was mortified, but my father was extremely forgiving.

Mrs Meyer's Nursery School on Hampstead Heath. I am 2nd from right in the back row, a bit pink after playing football (vigorously)

Towards the end of my time at Mrs Meyer's school, as a strapping four year-old, I was very daringly allowed to walk home on my own. This was on the grounds that it was just around the corner and did not involve crossing any roads. Nevertheless, in today's cautious society, this seems very high on the scale of 'can-do' encouragement. I was bursting with pride when I first came charging through the front door (which was always kept unlocked in those days).

This was well over a year after I had already cracked my first pun. The waiter's name in our holiday hotel was Carlos; Harry: "Has he lost his car?!" One bad pun deserves another, and the joyous art of writing limericks in church when the sermon is boring, and the appreciation of playing with words that, as TS Eliot suggests, 'move' and 'will not stay still', are (unlike missing limbs) all entirely genetic and gratefully inherited from my father.

It was time to go to 'big' school and my mother took me on my first day at the local New End Primary School on 7th September 1964. I was just over 5 years old and I was unwilling to let go of her hand. Some despicable teacher distracted me with two decoy flopsy bunnies and by the time I realised my mistake I spun round to see her glancing back regretfully over her shoulder as she slipped out of the school gate. She cried all the way home and I cried every morning at parting for four weeks or so but was very happy when collected, which they told my mother was a good sign.

I was too frightened to go out of the classroom into the playground at all, let alone when it was full of screaming children at playtime. Eventually my friends Jason and David took it on themselves to dare me to go a few steps out of the door, to touch that further and then even further bit of wall. I soon got the hang of it rather well, although I suffered further severe nerves when we graduated into the senior playground. The walls were daubed with simple graffiti, mostly the names of local football teams Arsenal and Chelsea. In 1968, the two biggest, nastiest boys at the school, Paul and Gary, both supported Chelsea. Basic self-protection was a good enough reason for me to do the same and I am eternally grateful to them as I have followed The Blues ever since. We always played football (vigorously) at playtime and particularly a game we called Paddle. This is where you had to kick the tennis ball between two agreed pillars in the wall and if you missed then you lost a life. I wasn't very good at Paddle, having a right foot shaped like a putter, although I did get unusual speed off my shin and ankle.

At school, the leg was nearly always an asset rather than a disadvantage. "I bet it will hurt more if I kick you than if you kick me" (NB remember to stand with the metal one nearest the challenger). The biography of Norman Croucher OBE, a mountain climber with two artificial legs, is similarly called *Shin Kicking Champion*.

I have no strong memory of being picked on or bullied because of my leg. My friends would gleefully ride their bikes over it to shock their mothers and I had an impressive collection of football stickers on it from the bubblegum packs. The disadvantage of the stickers was that they took the pink paint off when they peeled. This left silver blotches of bare metal that eventually qualified for a re-spray. The solid metal leg had a rather more mundane service when I was smaller, being perfect at picnics for cracking hard-boiled eggs.

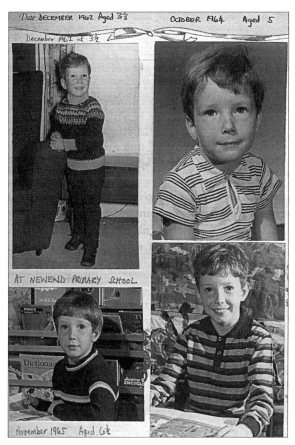

Growing in confidence in my school photographs from New End School, Hampstead

Horseplay

The artificial leg prevented me from serious injury several times in my childhood, and mostly from horses. My sister went through a horsey phase and I was the one nominated to go with her on the rides. I can't now remember whose "placid and friendly" horse kicked me. Joanna and I were sent to play with it and we were trying to lead it somewhere, I think, somewhere it clearly didn't want to go anyway. It was Joanna's idea that she would pull it and I would push it. Bad mistake. The horse understandably kicked the stupid seven year-old standing behind it. Luckily it connected with the thick leather corset I had on the old metal leg and I suffered only bruising. It wasn't really the next horse's fault either, that threw me off onto the gravel road when it jumped suddenly. But it certainly was the other bloody "placid and friendly" horse's fault that decided to have a roll as we rode across Lligwy beach in Anglesey. It just fancied it, clearly, and lay down on its side to squirm. Like the kicking incident, this could have been serious but fortunately again my leg came to the rescue as the horse rolled only on the metal bit and I escaped unscathed.

Following my sister on, or out from behind a horse was normal for my childhood. Joanna was, and continues to be, a confident and natural leader. She invented, directed and starred in all the plays we would perform as children at Christmas time. I remember a particularly imaginative one about a child who had to eat her way out of a Christmas pudding. In this play, Joanna got to be the child who had to eat her way out of a Christmas pudding and I got to be a sixpence (or was it a currant?). She also invented some great games. When we stayed with my grandmother in Dean we regularly went off on our own to play on the haystacks at a local farm. We built forts and dens and jumped from high places. We were sitting on a tractor when Joanna invented a game called "make up a song". Hers started "All I want is a room somewhere, far away from the cold night air..." and the chorus rang "Oh woooouldn't it be luvverly!" It was a great song, and I was dismayed that I couldn't make up a song on the spot that was as good as my big sister's. It was some years before I discovered that I had been done by that old bigger sibling trick of 'inventing' something from a film (*My Fair Lady* in this case) that they'd seen but you hadn't because you were too young. Then again, she did rescue me from a herd of stampeding cows, which were trying to take refuge from a storm under the same tree as me. Joanna bravely sashayed in, star-jumping and shouting: "Hoy hoy hoy", while I did my impression of a rabbit in a headlight.

Is He Musical?

My Baby Book records that from a very early age I would nod my head in time to music. It also says that I would bash away merrily on the piano keys before climbing onto them in search of other entertainment. I received a setback to loving the piano at home when, before I could read, Joanna pointed to the maker's name on the piano and asked me if I knew what it said. I shook my head. She traced along the gold letters and read out: "Harry wets his pants". I was upset, even though it was true at the time, but I soldiered on with my musical career and, aged 5, I picked out a tune on a piano for my first composition. No need for Beethoven to roll over, except perhaps in his grave.

At primary school I was selected to try out for violin lessons with an ancient Austrian man who came in to teach. Even though the left hand does the fancy bit with the strings on the finger board, the old boy judged that, because of my missing fingers, I could not hold the bow properly with my right hand and sent me promptly back to my classroom. I was tearful on my return, but it may have been the embarrassment and frustration of the rejection rather than the lifelong desire to play the violin. Years later we were given a small violin that could have been used by my children as they gained an interest in music... had I not hidden it in the loft. Was this my revenge against the old violin teacher? Or my reaction as a French Horn player to disdain a violin on principle? Or just my human instinct to protect myself from the excruciating noise of a learner violin at close quarters? I don't remember my parents being *too* upset at my exclusion from the violin class; we already had a deaf neighbour who played the violin, with the inevitably casual approach to tuning.

New End School photo – aged 10½

I next took up piano lessons. Every Thursday my teacher Rosemary Bonar picked me up from school. She drove a red Toyota and was just young enough to make it seem fantasy-worth for an early teenager. I did learn a few classical pieces, and I can still play some of them by ear today. But, without the physical capacity of ten fingers and the mental application to practise, I ended up learning a lot of Beatles tunes, which were more attractive. Miss Bonar, as I always knew her, was skilled at picking pieces that had a dominant left hand and a modest span in the right. Elton John or David Bowie? Too many notes! Missing two fingers on the right hand meant no chords that were too wide and with only one note in the middle, please, in the same way my typing requires no words with O, P or L in them because they are too far to the right.

The first piece I learned with Miss Bonar was the Welsh tune *All Through The Night*. The tune was in the left hand with a few basic chords in the right – perfect! I quickly learned it by heart and it once served as a massive relief for my parents. On holiday on a mountaintop in Switzerland we came across a boarded up house. Some boards had come adrift and several children were slipping into the deserted house, so Joanna and I followed them. After a while my parents were becoming a little uneasy that we hadn't been seen for some time, until suddenly the strains of *All Through The Night* came plonking out of the house from a piano I had found in the semi-darkness, and my parents knew that all was well.

These Legs Are Made For Walking (Allegedly)

You will hear some of my friends and relations suggesting that I don't like walking, as in 'going for a nice long walk'. It is true that I don't like getting wet and miserable walking in the rain. It is also true that I don't generally like the discomfort of picnics and having to share my lunch with insects. It is also true that the regular pounding of walking is most likely to develop a sore on the leg and so walking less is preventative against not being able to walk at all. Sometimes I think walks (and even long walks) can be fabulous.

When I was ten years old, I completed a 10-mile sponsored walk as a Cub Scout. I went with my American friend Paul, wearing his own blue Cub Scout uniform, up and down the hills of Hampstead. I remember we ran the last few hundred yards for the joy of completing the walk and then enjoyed an ice cream to celebrate.

A few years later I joined my sister and her friends on an Oxfam sponsored "Find the monuments". We had a Red Rover go-as-you-please bus ticket, planning to walk the bits where the buses didn't go. There were forty selected monuments dotted round central London, with a marshal positioned at each, and I learned a lot about the heritage of my city by getting my sponsor form stamped at the Peter Pan statue in Hyde Park and the Burghers of Calais outside the Houses of Parliament. However I was undone by Henry Moore's Locking Piece. The dodgy plan of the monuments, given out by Oxfam, failed to show that this monument was actually some way off the map to the south. We walked and walked, let down too by a Sunday bus service, until we finally found the flaming thing outside the Tate Gallery. My leg suffered, I was forced to give in to a blistered stump and frustratingly failed to complete the course. The following year, fore-armed with knowledge of where the monuments all were and accompanied by a gang of mates on our bicycles, we whizzed round the course in excellent time. The only moment of bother came when I nearly got myself run over in Exhibition Road, crossing towards the Albert Memorial at one of these new-fangled Pelican Crossings that neither I, nor the driver, seemed fully to understand.

Because the artificial foot is set up for standard heel and toe walking on flat ground it is less well designed for slopes and steps. Actually it is fine for going up but not for going down. The modern dynamic foot copes well with planting the toe on the mountainside, takes the strain and gives the spring upwards and onwards. It must be quite a hit to have the whole weight concentrated on the toe end, rather than the weight passing through this part of the foot on the way out of a normal stride. The old wooden feet would quickly give in and give way, but these days the plastic is robust and it copes in the same way with bounding upstairs (with no stubbed toes when you get the clearance wrong). When most people come down hills they point their toes like a ballet dancer to achieve maximum surface area of the foot on the mountainside and therefore maximum traction. With my fixed ankle I always lead with my heel, and by the time my foot is flat on the hillside my body is tilting forward alarmingly and the momentum is rapidly downwards. I therefore come down mountains (when I come) with my foot planted sideways across the slope. With no weedy flesh and bone ankle to turn, this is an effective non-slip way of digging the foot into the side of the slope. My very newest plastic foot, exclusive to this year's model, actually tilts and flattens sideways for the first time. Gripping stuff – and certainly no more call for the jokes about having legs of different length and therefore needing always to walk clockwise around mountains to keep both feet on the ground.

People point their toes coming down stairs too, but I always land on my heel. There is sometimes a distracting noise of breaking wind as the air seeps into the artificial leg's socket when the leg dangles in space over the lower stair and then the air is expelled when the weight comes down on it. Nowadays the hard heel on my leather 'work' shoes makes an almighty clang on metal escalators in the London Underground when I run for the Victoria Line, although this does help to clear the dawdling tourists out of the way. These legs are made for walking and that's just what they'll do.

Sent To Purgatory And Other School Journeys

We did plenty of walking on my two school journeys out of New End School. Only a year apart, they were poles apart in how I felt about them. The first was to Marchants Hill, near the Devil's Punchbowl in Surrey. It was more or less my first time away from home. Mum and Dad saw me onto the dreaded ILEA bare boneshaker bus and I'm not sure which of us was more upset. As we pulled away from the Old White Bear in Hampstead the staff handed out the barley sugars. This was said to combat travel sickness but it probably helped to quieten the whimpering. They had recently changed the classes at New End and I was in with a lot of older children that I didn't know. I was apprehensive of the older boys and girls and I felt like Harry no-mates.

The conditions at Marchants Hill, formerly an evacuation centre for English and Dutch youngsters during the Second World War, were basic (some would say primitive). It has recently been modernised, but in 2006 their web pages were still advertising:

> *"The timber-clad chalets at Marchants Hill are designed to accommodate a party of 40 – 50. Most chalets are divided into two large dormitories with five smaller rooms with washbasins for adults. Each chalet has its own night toilet, with the main toilet and shower blocks close by."*

Well, the term "chalet" is a brilliant bit of spin. It sounds cosy and efficiently Swiss, whereas I remember only massive wooden sheds filled with bare boards and tin bunks. I don't remember whether we were spoiled with an indoor "night toilet" but I do remember having to hop outside for a shower. Rumour had it that the camp commandant would allow us a change of underwear on a Wednesday – but we'd only be allowed to 'change them' with the urchins from Broxbourne, who were the aggressive occupiers of the other half of our shed. (This is an old Second World War joke in keeping with the camp's history.) In any case toilets were a bit of an issue for me at Marchants Hill because I was not yet "dry at night". This was a cause of some anxiety for me in strange surroundings, with strange people. I'd already declined the top bunk (for fear of accidentally dripping on my classmate) when we were setting up our beds. I had hoped to keep my personal problem personal, but the Hut Warden stood in the middle of the room and shouted: "Rubber sheet for Harry Wade".

We had timetabled sessions for writing home but my letters gave little away. I disclosed miserably on the second day that "I think I have stayed long enough here already" and the fact that I sent my love not only to Bracken, the dog, but also to my sister, must have shown my parents that I was feeling a little emotionally vulnerable. Short of news, in desperation my father sent me a questionnaire that urged me to fill in the blanks. This is an excellent ploy that I have used myself to get information out of my own children and I thoroughly recommend. "What is the best thing about it?" (playing football); "What is the worst thing?" (the food – especially the grey, slimy, bitter-tasting gruel that pretended to be porridge;) "Who are you sharing a bunk bed with?" (Martin). The flaw in the exercise was that I failed to send the questionnaire home and ended up delivering it by hand. During the week I became friends with Martin, whose best trick was to screw up his face and do a hilarious impression of an SS Stormtrooper. I remember telling him, as the bus headed homewards at the end of the week, quite how oddly under-excited I was at the prospect of the inevitably tearful reunion. I had gained a slice of independence and confidence, just from getting through it. But I was happy to be back in my own bed again (next door to the bathroom).

My bedwetting was cured by a machine that set off an alarm when it detected moisture. It consisted of a flexible silver square that was placed underneath the sheet in the "target region". It was wired up to a transformer and alarm unit and switched on at night. Any drop of water would make it go off. It came with an explanatory leaflet with cartoons for boys and girls. The boys got a military tale: the scout is out in the field, when he senses attack (i.e. I wee) he gets on the blower to HQ and the General sounds the alarm. The girls got the same thing, only performed by the Queen of the Fairies and her winged messenger. Anyway, having live electric wires under my genitals and the prospect of setting off a loud alarm were more than enough to scare me into consciousness before the scout had anything to phone home about.

The second school journey from New End could not have been a more different experience. Armed with confidence from the previous year and surrounded by my mates we all went on a real luxury coach to a hotel in Swanage. We had four to a room, with good facilities, and the food was very tasty (apart from when my best mate Keith shook the ketchup bottle without the lid on properly, with hilarious but disastrous consequences). I still didn't write many letters home and then only sent love to the dog. We had a great time playing football – vigorously – on Maiden Castle, at Bovington Tank Museum and Old Harry Rocks (and he still does) and I came back with loads of photos that all seemed to feature Miss Devlin, the pretty student teacher. I was definitely growing up.

My best friend Keith, another Chelsea fan

Keith was a buck-toothed boy with blue eyes that sparkled and crinkled when we giggled together. He was also rather precocious in his awareness of females, given that the boys mainly ignored the girls and vice versa at this stage of different development. It was certainly him who started the giggling at the saucy part of the film *The Charge of the Light Brigade*. It was my birthday party treat, but once all seven of us boys were sniggering off our cinema seats my parents became unusually ratty. Keith was also another Chelsea fan and his dad took us to our first ever live Chelsea game – home to Southampton. We stood on the terraces opposite the Shed End and the history books say the match finished 2-2. However the only incidents I can remember now are when Southampton forward Ron Davies came sprinting towards us, only to be flagged offside, and when I got bruising on my bottom when the crowd surged forward and I got trampled on. Maybe this was one of the goals I missed? Keith and I stayed up late, listening to Chelsea winning the European Cup-Winners' Cup in 1971, glued to the radio on top of the fridge; and we'd stayed up even later at his house to watch the moon landing (officially voted the 20th Century's most memorable "Where were you when..." moment).

In The Swim

I'm reasonably sure it was my charm, virtue and leadership qualities that got me the honour of being the first child into the new swimming pool at New End Primary School, rather than some flimsy favour. On the other hand, for years I wondered, when things went well at school, if it wasn't because of me, but because my parents and teachers teamed up to somehow make it ok for the kid with one leg. I have no evidence for this suggestion, so case never proven, but the occasional doubt was ultimately not good for the self-esteem. In fact I believe my leg and hand are almost never in other people's consciousness to the same extent as they are in mine; the less I notice them, the less everyone else will notice them too.

In the brand new pool in a New End School classroom, 3rd from right

I was taught to swim, aged 6, by Mr Buchstan, assisted by a tattooed man called Mike, and I loved them both. My mother records for April 1966: "Can swim and dive (after lessons at Swiss Cottage Baths) but can't quite breathe yet, except when swimming on his back". I passed my gold life-saving badge and went on to represent my house at the senior school swimming gala. I used to dive off the top board at the baths; I would clamber up the ladder using my right knee and then hop to the end. It was a challenge to keep balance and not to wobble at the point of diving, but the health and safety executive did away with public diving boards because people landed on other swimmers or did spectacular belly-flops. To have a rose-flushed chest or back from top bombing was quite a badge of honour. I still really enjoy coming down the water slides at places like Centre Parcs; what I really hate is hopping up the staircases to get to them. It is very tiring on the calf muscles. What we need is someone to invent a waterproof escalator, or a ski lift that pulls or carries you up and then lets you slide down when ready.

Life-saving exams are an interesting quandary for people with artificial limbs that I can't remember now how we resolved. The point is that you pretend that you are just walking along when you hear a distress call. So you jump in with your clothes on, take them off and then rescue someone nearby. So, do you have to jump in with your leg on and take that off as well as your clothes? Or are you allowed to hop to the pool and pretend that this is how you are likely to be when you see someone drowning? Actually, I imagine Dr J____ would have been apoplectic if I had jumped in a swimming pool with my leg on, so I assume I was allowed to start legless.

It's A Beach

The first time I remember my foot falling off was when my family were on summer holidays in Brittany. I must have been 8 or 9 when I was running after the ball on a beach and I fell flat on my face. I assumed I had stepped in a hole, but in fact the foot had come clean off and was dangling from my sock. Northern Breton beach resorts in the late Sixties were ill-equipped to deal with prosthetic repairs and we ended up taking the leg to the local blacksmith. He put a crude Frankenstein-style bolt through the whole thing, which then looked a bit like Ben Hur's chariot.

Beaches are not very easy places for artificial limb users. I love to swim in the sea and the salt water is very good for the day to day sores and abrasions on the stump that don't normally see the light of day. Hopping to the water can be tricky though. A flat beach with the tide out and the sand in picturesque wrinkles is like having your instep beaten with a stick, not to mention exhausting hopping over a long distance. Slippery seaweed is a nightmare as well as sharp shells and stones. When you've hopped back over all these, past the inquisitive tourists, your leg is full of sand and rubs like sandpaper.

Probably good to get the whinge over early, because beaches really are the place I feel most disadvantaged with only one leg. You can't snorkel properly because you've only got one flipper; the pedalos are fearfully hard work and go round in circles; and I'm sad to miss out on the spontaneous paddle. Even without the prospect of a scarlet-faced Dr J____, salt water rots and rusts artificial legs; so it's NO PADDLING – unless of course you've brought your 'sea-leg'.

Most artificial limb-wearers have a leg for best and another as a spare. If you don't tell Dr J____, or equivalent, you can take the spare with you on the beach holiday and not mind so much if the salt, sand and maybe even water get in the joints. In Brittany that year as a child, I only had the one leg as I was growing so fast that the old one simply didn't fit. Nowadays I do have a sea-leg. It was really important for me as a dad with young children to be able to play with them actively on a beach. An extra leg may take up a lot of space in a suitcase, and the metal core looks like a rifle on the x-rays at the airport, but the freedom to be a beach biped is brilliant.

GROWING UP

HIGHER EDUCATION introduced more physical activity to challenge the fleshy and the synthetic bits of my legs. It also introduced more psychological activity, like most teenagers, on how I felt about my body, and how was I likely to get to feel someone else's body?

At best, I felt most heroic with my metal leg in my school teenage years. My secondary education was at a state grammar called William Ellis School. I gave a talk to the full assembly of 600 boys about how an artificial leg works and plonked my spare leg up on the headmaster's lectern. I spent several happy summers with my older cousins in Ilkley and their children always called it my 'bionic' leg. This felt great as *The Bionic Man* was a TV series of the time featuring a hero who was destroyed by criminals but reconstructed to see justice done. "We have the technology," said the voiceover, and I was the similarly metal-clad force for good. *The Terminator* was less good for the bionic image.

Modelling the William Ellis School uniform, 1970
The cap lasted about 3 days

I cycled to school every day over Hampstead Heath, where a good speed meant not getting caught by Jock the park keeper. Parliament Hill, one of the highest points in North London, rose directly between my house and my school. If I was feeling particularly energetic I would stand on the pedals and heave myself up to the summit. This gave a fabulous view of central London, as enjoyed rather less by Catesby and the other Gunpowder Plotters, and a wonderful breakneck freewheel for half a mile down to the ponds. Mostly, however, discretion is the better part of valour and I went round the side.

One day I was cycling outside our house when I was attacked by the dog from across the road, called Jakoba. It always hated cyclists and this was reciprocated. Out of nowhere, Jakoba barked and darted out as I cycled past. She bit me on the leg and yelped. Lying on the pavement were two teeth... and she was never known to attack a bicycle again. More protection comes from always pushing my bike on the right hand side. What a great shield a metal leg is against those deeply painful bruises caused by the pedals knocking against the ankle or shin.

The bicycle gang in the back yard with the Stringer boys

I was "the biter bit" a few years later when I was fending off a friend when playing bicycle football. I stuck out my armoured leg, but caught it in the spokes of their back wheel. With a clatter the leg was pulled straight off, down the trouser leg and bounced on the tarmac. This seriously inhibited my ability to pedal, but I was able to freewheel back to pick it up and pop it back on.

My best mate for most of my time at William Ellis was Nick Hackett. I would call for him every morning and we would cycle the last bit of the journey in formation like the Red Arrows. We spent five years together in and out of school and my leg was never an issue for us. He first remembers me when he sat next to me in a P.E. lesson when we were about 12 years old. He recalls noticing a large hole in my leg, peeping out between my sock and the tracksuit trousers that I always wore. He helpfully pointed it out to me, in case I hadn't noticed it, so I told him it was a ventilation hole for my metal leg. This came as a bit of a surprise to him, as he didn't know I had a metal leg, but probably not as surprising as it would have been for me if I hadn't known that I had a large hole in my leg.

All the Hackett family, with a strong connection to Ballydehob in County Cork, were very easy-going and relaxed. They were so relaxed that they did not believe in answering the phone until they were absolutely ready. I complained once that Nick had not answered the phone, even though I knew he was at home. He explained that he had heard the phone ring but by the time he had finished frying an egg for his breakfast, buttering the toast and then eating it... I had rung off. My fault entirely. He was also relaxed when my wooden foot gave way as we were running for a bus together, but he was on-the-ball enough to stop the bus and deliver the memorable line: "Please can you wait a minute because my friend's foot has fallen off?" The bus driver probably had a stiff drink when he got back to the depot.

I had extra thick patches on my corduroys when Nick and I played Subbuteo all weekend and the big metal knee hinges did their worst. I couldn't feel the helpless plastic player under me until I heard the snap of Larry Lightning, the Willoughby Wanderers flying winger, calling for the wet sponge and the tube of Uhu glue. Up in the loft I still have the box of fantasy programmes I made including those crunch games: Willoughby Wanderers vs Avenue South End, Willoughby Wanderers vs Goldhurst Growlers and, the big one, Willoughby Wanderers vs Hackett's Hornets, which actually happened every weekend.

Manager Harry Wade, aged 12 ½, gave the first generation of Willoughby Wanderers players alliterative but rather literal names. The exciting forward line, playing 4-2-4 alongside Larry Lightning, included Nigel Netbuster and the (inevitably) free-scoring Harry Header. Slightly more mundane, at the back were Tim Tackler, Dan Defender and the plodding Simon Centre-half. The programmes had hand-drawn pictures of just a few of Harry Header's goals from the imaginary game the previous week. They often had interviews with key figures from the club – mostly manager Harry Wade – and sometimes features on what Calvin Clearance got up to on his day off. Crucially, they faithfully reproduced the stern warnings that were found in the real Chelsea programmes of the day: "Boys! Stay off the pitch!" Unfortunately Willoughby Wanderers vs Hackett's Hornets still suffered from pitch invasions, when someone let the dog in and she became excited to see Nick and I already lying on the ground ready to play.

I had to make up everyone else's team to furnish the latest in the series of programmes that I loved to bash out on the old typewriter in our house. My mother never played Subbuteo in her life, but I consulted her on the name of her team, Diana's Devils, and then filled it with suitable Welshmen to reflect her origins. At least Nick picked his own Hackett's Hornets team for me to put in a programme.

I was a bit sceptical about his team to begin with. He had a couple of names like my boys in Hookey Hackett and the keeper Nicky Fumble. But the rest of his team were made up of off-beat characters like Eeyore, Hai Karate and That's Bass. However, as we grew older, the Hackett's Hornets team was able to keep its media-savvy cool whereas the old Willoughby Wanderers team began to sound a bit embarrassingly young. In a transformation worthy of the Abramovich era at Chelsea, anyone with a name that started with the same letter as his surname was sacked. Harry Header, despite knocking in six goals against Barnet Bangers, was replaced in the number 10 shirt overnight by Don Galloway. All the new WW players had names that sounded like they had both a lantern jaw and a TV show of their own. I continued to make a few programmes with the second generation Willoughby Wanderers, but somehow the joy had gone out of it. Eventually I graduated onto solo games of Subbuteo cricket, where my old school mates like Nick anchored the fantasy Gentlemen XI against a completely new set of players called the Ladies XI. Now that was scary, because we didn't really know anything about their form or statistics.

Long hair was 'in' for me and Nick Hackett, 1974

Red Roving We Will Go

Every summer, as a ritual, Nick and I would have a day on the buses. The annual Red Rover outing had no particular purpose, other than the joy of jumping on and off a lot just because we could. We would set ourselves targets, such as going on all the buses with single figure numbers: the No 1 at Waterloo, the No. 2 to Marble Arch and the No. 3 all the way south to the terminus at Crystal Palace, where it would turn round and come back again. This last one looks like a particular waste of time but seemed to stick in our schedule every year, probably for the sheer companionability of the time spent chatting together. There were other fixtures in the day, such as lunch at Lyons Corner House by Westminster Bridge. I was disappointed not to be awarded a Blue Peter Badge despite my diligent and interesting letter to them about the number of yoghurts past their sell-by date at Lyons, shortly after the new labelling concept had been introduced. I don't think this was the reason that this once-famous London institution closed down.

Another popular fixture on the Red Rover route (via the No. 72) was to call in at BBC Television Centre in Shepherds Bush to see my dad. Dad had risen to Head of Television Script Unit, bringing on talents such as Willy Russell, Colin Welland and Alan Bleasdale. However his name was mud when we called in unexpectedly and caught him having a crafty smoke. I had very strict rules about not smoking having already driven my mother to abandon the habit by exaggerated coughing; she only smoked about two a day to emulate the glamorous Canadian woman down the road. Dad claims it wasn't a crafty smoke but compulsory for those creative meetings with budding writers, though I still seem to remember his guilty expression when we burst in.

Dad would sometimes take us for a lemonade in the BBC canteen. This gave an amazing opportunity to see TV stars in the flesh. I got the autograph of Wendy Craig and one of my greatest claims to fame was to share a lift with Harry Secombe (quite a feat). The absolute highlight was meeting Eric Morecambe. I stood next to this comedy genius as my dad piped up: "My son would like to shake your hand". "I'll shake anything" he replied, made light of the lipstick smudge on his collar and then asked if I was going to their show that night. He promptly fished out a ticket for the studio recording of *The Morecambe & Wise Show* (the Egyptian one with Glenda Jackson) for that night. Eric and Ernie did their own warm-up of the studio audience, where some employed old lags like Barry Cryer to do it for them. Dad managed to slip into the audience carrying his BBC employee's free copy of the *Radio Times*. As a moving object he attracted Eric's attention, who promptly said: "Good evening sir, I see you've brought your own comic – wa-hey!"

The Morecambe & Wise Show was not the first recording I had seen at Television Centre. Dad was also able to slip Joanna and me into a recording of Blue Peter and so we met Valerie Singleton and John Noakes and were personally given a Blue Peter Badge. I didn't complain about not getting one for the letter about the yoghurts. I nearly achieved another claim to fame of being savaged by Blue Peter dog Petra. This ageing Alsatian did not take kindly to two kids suddenly appearing over the top of her pen in the studio and made a snapping attack. No damage done, but this does give credence to the story that the pets were drugged to keep them from wandering off or committing indiscretions with the guests.

Different-Shaped Balls – Rugby/Football

I loved to play football (vigorously) as a boy. At 10, as Chelsea legend Bobby Tambling, I would bang 100 goals onto the tin garage door in the yard behind our house, although it must have driven the neighbours potty. But, apart from in the playground, William Ellis School only played rugby and not football.

Not expected to wear rugby shorts and later banned for being too dangerous

However, my rugby career at school was a short one. I struggled to get enthusiastic about putting my face near someone's flailing boot and this was overtaken by others' unwillingness to put their faces near a flailing metal leg. Even an expert tackler needs to hit the flesh bit of the opponent's leg with their collarbone, and when the fleshy bit isn't fleshy it hurts. For me there was the added disadvantage that, when pulled in a tackle, my leg was likely to slip off. The bonus side of this happened once when I was tackled by the school rugby captain as I approached the try line and, with a swish and a slight pop I hopped over the line while the tackler was left clutching the empty leg. No doubt that's why he complained to the authorities that I was too dangerous to play with and I was banned. Horrid, rough game rugby anyway...

Keen to play football elsewhere, at 15 I would cycle to Primrose Hill to play in a regular Sunday morning kickabout with Nick, Marc-Henri and a motley bunch of others who gathered and departed in simple faith that most of us would be there again next week. Fred, the long-haired talented one in the Juventus shirt, and Bob, the more mundane clogger in the white rugby shirt, were typical of the others who were usually older than us and rather more skilful. I had a cultured left foot and an L-shaped right one. I remember one glorious turn, where I twisted on my left foot and "literally" hooked the ball down at an impossible angle, leaving Fred and another stranded. However most weeks it was a constant struggle to stay out of goal. I did have one golden morning between the posts where everything stuck in my hands or bounced away off various parts of the body. We won 9-2 where normally it was 7-6. I was man of the match, but I was also stuck in goal for weeks afterwards.

I do my impression of Bozzie the beagle with Marc-Henri and Nick Hackett

Football clubs have been slow to understand the spectrum of needs of fans with disabilities, although this has worked to my advantage on occasions. I remember the days when there used to be a ring of pale blue invalid carriages parked round the running track at Stamford Bridge. Many of the Chelsea players in the mid-70s would use them for target practice – at least I assume that was why they so rarely put the ball in the goal but instead peppered the surround. Declaring a disability at a football ground was also a way to get a ticket when there weren't any left and to get a great seat with loads of legroom. I was almost on the grass right behind the goal at Tottenham (also at risk from wayward shooting) and right at pitch-side (with three alleged 'helpers') in the ambulant disabled seats, for disabled people who can walk a bit, for an England game in Leicester. Then again, mainly because I am so tall, I really don't fit into some seats that are on general sale. In 2009, the seats in Chelsea's ageing East Stand are still too tight for me to sit straight, although at least the plastic ridge on the seat in front doesn't hurt when it digs into the artificial leg.

Blackmail Glenn Hoddle

I have already said that, when Dr J_____ isn't looking, you can use your spare artificial leg as a 'sea-leg' – i.e. one you can take in the sea when it doesn't matter about salt corrosion and it going rusty. But the very best use of a sea-leg is to blackmail Glenn Hoddle. In 1992 I was walking across a car park of a zoo in Nice (as you do) when who should I see in a Swindon Town tee-shirt but the big-chinned one himself. Even before he started the revolution at Chelsea FC, Hoddle was a hero whether you supported Spurs or not. I asked him for his autograph and he agreed, but I was short of something to sign. In desperation I asked if he'd sign my spare artificial leg. We had an exchange as I moved to the car along the lines of: "Where do you keep it?" "In the boot" which even made old Glenn laugh. "I've never signed one of these before!" he quipped and we all guffawed politely. When he took Chelsea to the FA Cup final in 1994 I thought about writing to him to plead for tickets on the grounds that mine was the only artificial leg he had ever signed and he surely must have taken advantage of this in his developing after-dinner speaking career. I didn't write the letter and anyway we lost 4-0, so probably one to forget.

The real moment came for the "Hoddle signs artificial leg in Nice Zoo car park shock!" was a few years later. In 1999 Hoddle lost his job as England manager chiefly for some ill-judged remarks about disabled people. Something along the lines of disability being a punishment for wrong-doings in a previous life. For a few days at the height of the media storm around this offensive statement, I had sitting in my loft an autographed prosthetic, a fabulous scoop worth £20,000 of any tabloid's money surely? But in the time it took for me to decide whether I would say "Hoddle spat at me while he signed my leg" (and look miserable in the photo) or "Hoddle was a hero and we laughed and joked together about positive images for disabled people" (and look happy in the photo) – the moment for tabloid fame and fortune passed me by. I've still got the leg he signed, and I should probably mount it like a stag's head on the wall, but it got a bit damp in the loft and is a little mildewy now.

The only artificial leg ever signed by Glenn Hoddle

Meanwhile, back at William Ellis, another school activity were the dreaded P.E. lessons when we did gymnastics. I did pass my bronze BAGA award (naturally we called it "Bugger awards"), which included flying forward rolls and walking along a high beam. I remember the P.E. teacher 'Daphne' (why did we call him that?) Brewer praising my courage for taking it on and shouting at all the others to keep their eyes up and to concentrate on the feel of the beam under their plimsolls. It is a lot easier to balance when you don't look down, but for me it was the only way of telling if the foot was still on the beam. A ridiculous amount of P.E. lessons were spent doing cross-country runs. This took advantage of William Ellis School's favourable location on Hampstead Heath, but otherwise seemed like gratuitous cruelty to the boys. I am delighted to say that I never, ever had to endure that soggy trudge, as I put down an early marker and got out of cross-country by using my leg as an excuse. Hooray for having one leg!

LEARNING AND PERFORMING

I PASSED NINE GCE 'O' Levels at William Ellis. This includes spoken English (my favourite), where I got a top A following a presentation about my artificial leg. I spoke about it in my French Oral too, having mugged up the vocabulary about *une jambe artificiele*, to be useful later in the ski-hire shop.

We were not allowed to study English Literature 'O' Level as the head of English, W.I. (Paddy) Browne, thought it would put people off literature for life. In truth I think it means that some of my early classmates will never have knowingly read or heard a word of Shakespeare in their lives. Apart from the usual collection of subjects, I really enjoyed Latin and Ancient Greek. They have been invaluable for picking up other classical languages like French, Italian and Spanish and for improving spelling in English. Much of the enjoyment was due to the excellent teacher Joe Harvey, who made the learning such fun. He organised 'classics trips' to significant Roman places that also involved sugar on the pill of a trip to the seaside: Colchester (Camulodunum) and Bath (Aquae Sulis) followed respectively by Clacton (Dodgems) and Weston-super-Mare (Mini Golf). We started with the simple nouns and regular verbs, I particularly remember translating early on: "The sailors chased the boys into the sea", which caused some amusement in an all-boys school. We went on to study Homer, but sadly I was the Simpson of the class. The only line of Ancient Greek I can still remember is the rudest phrase Joe was prepared to teach us: "βαλ εσ κορακας", which means "throw yourself to the crows". I still use it frequently.

Joe Harvey also taught me most of the Latin I ever learned. Unfortunately we lost him as a teacher for 'O' Level classes and he was replaced by a camp Canadian who simply could not hold the class. We started with simple imitations of his accent and distinctive pronunciation of the catchphrase: "canjagate the vurrrrrb". But what a time we had that day in class 3G! Within fifteen minutes of the start of the lesson, all 32 of us were lifting the wooden lids of our desks, sticking our heads in and mooing. This may sound anti-social now but I assure you it was completely the right thing to do at the time. The teacher left the room and returned briefly to declare "This class has a number of bastards in it!" before leaving for the day. We were shocked and elated, and it was well worth my only (class) detention. My only individual detention came with just a few days left of the Upper Sixth. I was vice-head boy, chatting to the physics teacher Mike Detheridge, who discovered that I had never had a detention. He immediately put me in the book, with the reason "Never had one", although fortunately I was not required to stay behind after school for an hour.

Another super, inspirational teacher for me was Hugh Black-Hawkins. He was my sixth form tutor and also taught English Lit to packed classes. Over the years students would choose Chemistry, Physics and English, or in essence English plus whatever they were really good at or wanted to study later.

Hugh had the confidence and charisma to front a class and galvanise even the most reluctant into participation. His teaching style included the relatively immoral and indecent and utterly provocative but he had the perfect judgement to stay the right side of illegal. He knew the perfect line to hook 16 year-old boys into literature: sex. We were introduced to the phallic symbol. Once we knew where to look for it, every English lesson became an enthusiastic game of 'hunt the symbol'. He hit us early with Browning's yawningly slushy poem *Meeting at night*.

The grey sea and the long black land;
And the yellow half-moon large and low;
And the startled little waves that leap
In fiery ringlets from their sleep,
As I gain the cove with pushing prow,
And quench its speed i' the slush sand.

Then a mile of warm sea-scented beach;
Three fields to cross till a farm appears;
A tap at the pane, the quick sharp scratch
And blue spurt of a lighted match,
And a voice less loud, thro' its joys and fears,
Than the two hearts beating each to each!

The plot is that a romantic man rows onto a beach and crosses some fields before knocking on the window of his sweetheart's farmhouse. She lights a lamp and he holds her in his arms. Wrong!! It's all about sex. Half-moon – breasts; little waves of sexual arousal; pushing prow – say no more (not a boat); spurt of orgasmic lust and too tired to talk afterwards as they lay belly to belly. My mother was appalled but I went on to study it to degree level. By this I mean English literature in general, rather than exclusively the phallic symbol – which remained more of a hobby.

We had combined classes with the young ladies from Camden Girls School. They were trained in the full-frontal romanticism of their teacher Mrs Kellaway and our varying styles led to clashes. We studied the poetry of TS Eliot. The fact that his name is an anagram of 'toilets' probably struck a chord with the Camden girls as a comment on our approach to great literature. Star pupil Louise Radinger was due to treat us one lesson to a dramatic rendition. She felt under the weather that day but, undeterred, Mrs Kellaway rang her and bizarrely we all clustered round the phone to hear the slightly distorted performance of The Hollow Men (did they mean us?). "Alas!" she sighed, as we were "leaning together, headpiece filled with straw" still trying to get sex into everything. We fell out with the girls, who also included budding actress Emma Thompson, over The Wasteland. Eliot describes the river in the morning after the night before:

The river bears no empty bottles, sandwich papers,
Silk handkerchiefs, cardboard boxes, cigarette ends
Or other testimonies of summer nights.

The boys all *knew* that "other testimonies of summer nights" obviously meant 'used condoms', but the girls all agreed that it clearly meant 'picnic basket'. Never was the gender dividing line more clearly drawn.

Hugh also reintroduced to William Ellis the school play. His first effort was *Much Ado About Nothing*. Hugh set it in pre-war Edwardian England, long before the Royal Shakespeare Company had the same idea. Furthermore he brought in girls from the convent school across the road to balance out the cast from our all-boys school. This made appearing in the play and turning up for as many rehearsals as possible very attractive. Hugh had the inspiration to introduce devices to entertain the audience during the dull but important bits of plot. For when the action flagged, he recruited a wild red-haired boy in the new role of gardener to chase a pretty assistant gardener across the stage like Benny Hill. Much to Hugh's credit, a number of the staff joined in to play the comedy parts of Dogberry and the Watch. Some were genuinely funny, some were funny because they thought they were funnier and some were funny because they couldn't work out why they were funny. "How if the nurse be asleep and will not hear us?" bellowed the barrel-chested maths teacher. Everyone trusted Hugh to the extent that it was safe enough for the maths teacher, who had the reputation for being a little slow-witted, to overact being totally slow-witted. This was his only line and he never understood why it brought the house down, but he complied with the roars for an encore.

In *Much Ado* I was type-cast (not) as Friar Francis, the wise and cunning vicar. The Friar's only significant scene is when he comes up with the plan to pretend the girl has died in order to make the boy see what he is missing. I paced around my bedroom trying to memorise one of the biggest blocks of speech in the play. I can still reproduce most of it today:

"What we have we prize not to its worth while we enjoy it, but, being lacked and lost, why then we rack the value, then we find the virtue that possession would not show us whilst it was ours".

This can go down well at parties but the repetition is rarely appreciated by my close family. However the universal truth the speech contains, to value what you have when you actually have it, has become a key part of my philosophy. Or as Joni Mitchell said: "You don't know what you got till it's gone". I see it applying to far more than mere possessions. It applies to valuing one's health and wellbeing too. Two legs may be better than one, but one leg has served me very well and is surely better than no legs.

Meanwhile back to the play and, disastrously, the virtuous vicar didn't get to dance in the frolicking finale, whereas my mate Nick had no lines to remember and still got to dance the bunny-hop with sexy convent queen Carmen Khan. *Much Ado* certainly built my confidence to appear and speak in public but, apart from a few stolen kisses at the production party, it failed to bring me any prolonged contact with the opposite sex.

Hugh's second school play was an ambitious co-production, again with the convent school across the road. We used their hall to stage it, as the backstage facilities were better. Our physics department built the set and their art department painted it – a liaison that ended in the romance and marriage of the respective heads of department.

We performed *King Arthur*, with words by John Dryden and music by Henry Purcell. This ancient play had the potential to be deadly dull, but again Hugh's inspiration delivered a spectacular triumph. Period dress saw us boys struggling to avoid ladders in our tights. I was particularly self-conscious as the white stockings showed the bulbous contours of my dented metal leg and it looked blotchy where the patches of silver revealed the peeled-off paint. Nick was legendary with his one liner: "Hark a trumpet, it sounds a parley" and we all cupped our ears and lurched in unison to stage left.

The physics department's greatest moment featured lowering Venus down onto the stage in her shell as a stunning finale. Venus was played by the luscious biology teacher in a flimsy toga – thus fulfilling the fantasies of a high percentage of William Ellis boys, and probably Hugh himself (a recurring theme in his later productions).

Literary ears: I am harking centre stage, flanked by Sean French and Mark Mazower
Nick Hackett harks on behind

My only other juvenile acting experience came in a film about attitudes to mental health. It was a short educational film about a boy's uncle about to come out of hospital to live with the family. We were paid the princely sum of £50 cash to learn our lines and learn not to look into the camera.

We were recruited to play the boy's ignorant mates and we spent a day or so hanging around the alleyways of West Hampstead on our bicycles. I was asked to rough up my accent a bit to enhance my sense of ignorance. My best line was quite a long one and the accent did not hold up very well: "Wewll oi fink sum peepul loike that are often more frightened of you than you are of them" – starting very cockney and ending rather Hampstead. This is a bit ironic considering I had a broad cockney accent aged 10, to the point that my parents were concerned for my prospects! Anyway, they left in the take featuring the dwindling accent. They also left in another take where the camera panned from me over to the star. I was supposed to move from sitting on the back of my bike up onto the saddle. As I swung my leg over, I caught the neck of my jeans on the back of the saddle and (if you happen to be looking at me rather than at the star) you will clearly see my eyes crossing slightly.

So I suffered for my art, but I bought a new camera with the £50. We were invited for the first showing of the finished film. A good part of it features the star boy cycling around looking thoughtful with the subtle soundtrack of Pink Floyd's *Brain Damage*. It was my first taste of the artifice of film and TV as his journey looked like a straight line in the film but really jumped erratically around the local streets I knew so well. Many years later a friend's brother, who was training to be a doctor, reported a sighting of me in the film as part of the mental health module. And maybe it is still out there?

On the film set with Aaron (left) I moodily contemplate the saddle that will cause me pain

Taking Your Clothes Off In Public

If you have a knee, and you wear trousers, there is a reasonable chance that out on the street many people will not know that you have one leg unless you tell them; when you go swimming, you leave all pretence along with the leg in the dressing room. I prefer not to be seen as disabled. This seems to have worsened with age.

Having one leg in a swimming pool or on a beach is probably like having big breasts. It is not given quite the same "fwor factor" by the tabloids, but people find it really hard not to stare. I find myself eyeballing them thinking: "Keep those eyes up to mine... don't drop the stare", but inevitably the eyes flicker down, and you notice even though they think they got away with it. Some people in celebrity life enjoy being stared at, but I don't. It makes me self-conscious. I completely understand curiosity and, if I'm in the mood, I am ok with straight questions; but I don't like the furtive flickers.

Not suffering at all on a French beach

When I was 16 I was friends with a girl called Sara. She had been a good swimmer but lost a leg to bone disease and hadn't swum since. I agreed to join her in Camden's 'special' swimming sessions. Looking back it was like *One flew over the cuckoo's nest* with a grey municipal busload of people with a myriad of special needs trundling through the borough. It was fantastic that Sara started to swim again, and I didn't mind the free swimming at all; I was a bit spooked by the fellow-swimmers with learning disabilities, for whom curiosity about my leg meant 'have a feel'; and I was completely freaked out by being part of the public parade of the disabled as the bus completed the mighty loop to pick up and drop off. "Here is Harry Wade with a bunch of other disabled people!" There was no chance for me to convince the bus bystanders how individual and able I was – nor was there, of course, for anyone else for that matter. Sara and I were good friends, but when romance reared its head I backed out. I didn't want anyone to think that we were together just because we both had disabilities. I didn't particularly like the way she kissed either...but I have always felt guilty about letting her down.

In fishing terms, the most spectacular catch was inevitably 'the one that got away'. Actually they pretty much all got away, but the one I fished most hopefully but hopelessly for was Amanda G_____. She was in my sister's form at school and had been to our house. She was in my tennis coaching set and once asked me if I would be her partner in the tournament, but then it all went a bit quiet. She was very, very pretty. I had a real crush on her. She had a poem published in their school magazine; I learned it by heart and suddenly started using the phrase 'figment of my imagination' rather too much. My mother started teasing me by testing me on my Latin homework and asking me what the gerund (or something) 'fit to be loved' was... The answer is (of course) 'Amanda' and I flushed scarlet and shouted at her. I even took a bus to Pimlico to hang, casually, around the trendy shop where she worked. After six laps of the wicker baskets and perfumed candles it appeared that she wasn't working that Saturday and when challenged by another member of staff I fled back to the bus stop. It didn't work out for us. Amanda married well and became a socialite success, but she definitely didn't win the tennis tournament that year.

I talked over the Sara and the Amanda issue and the rest of the universe with Nick. "Plenty more fish in the sea, mate" was encouraging to hear for an aching hormonal 16-year-old.

Nick and his family always spent the summer in Ireland. We wrote long letters to each other that Nick's local postman traditionally always read first, which meant that we couldn't discuss anything very personal. The postie knocked on the door one summer bringing the much-awaited envelopes with the O level results for Nick and his twin sister Sue. "Congratulations, Mrs Hackett, they've both done very well, especially Nick's A grades in Physics and Chemistry", he announced.

The main honourable mention for Sue Hackett is that she was charitable enough to be the other participant in my first 'proper' kiss. Everyone at the party was probably stoned apart from me, so I could have set fire to the curtains or juggled with the best china and no-one would have remembered a thing. So my heartfelt thanks to Sue, but she didn't count as the right fish in the right sea either.

Little Acorns And Little Arrows

Much to my amazement, and delight, I did get lucky angling in Anglesey. In Nick's Irish absence I signed up to volunteer on a National Trust Acorn Camp with another school friend Dave. Dave and I were dominant key members of the music class. His father was a professional musician although Dave's chances of following him with his viola were hampered by his rugged rugby-player's wrists and he is now a successful distributor of motorcycle oil. Acorn Camps attracted young people to do maintenance or restorative work on NT properties. One particularly attractive young person on this Acorn Camp in Plas Newydd, Anglesey, was Louise. She had pretty blue eyes, sang sweetly to her guitar and laughed at my jokes. That was good enough for me. "Is she a good kisser?" asked Dave, who had apparently been exercising in a similar way with Gillie from Kent. Apart from my swift sampler with Sue, I really had no scale on which to assess a 'good kisser'. In truth, any kisser was a good kisser for me, so Louise definitely was.

We had a task at Plas Newydd to restore the original carriageway that ran up to the old house on the Menai Straits. A layer of earth about 20 cms thick had settled all along the carriageway, covered in weeds and grass. It was quite hard work chopping away at the earth and piling it up for disposal. On about the third day we discovered that if several of us slipped our spades underneath the leading edge of the weed blanket we could not only lift it but roll it up like a carpet. We hit our daily progress targets with ease. This left more time for 'conversation'.

But while the work was getting easier, the romance was getting more complicated. Dave and I had just finished the Lower Sixth form, Year 12 in new money, as had Louise, but Gillie had just done A Levels. Both girls were older than we were and we figured that they would not be interested in us if we were their juniors. So we lied. Yes, we'd just finished A Levels too, filling in university entrance papers, wondering what to do in our year off, etc.

My romance with Louise blossomed and we held hands and kissed a lot. One of the Christmas set pieces that Joanna and I performed together as children was *Little Arrows* by Leapy Lee, complete with the endearing "doo-do-do-doo" at the end of each line. I certainly had cupid's arrows in my clothing and in my hair for the first Real Thing with Louise. Gillie and Dave had a nice time too. Louise and I parted wistfully at the end of the week and we all agreed to stay in touch. The only thing Dave and I failed to do was tell them how old we really were.

When we got home, Dave and I discussed how we went forward with the girls from here. Nick's postman asked him what he thought I should do. We ended up writing a letter to our holiday romances, coming clean on our ages and hoping to see them again. Gillie turned out to be otherwise engaged (and later otherwise married) to a longstanding love called Phil. Wearing Dave's jumper on cold nights in Anglesey did not change her commitment to her hometown boy. Dave angrily blamed me for luring him into the age artifice that gave Gillie a further reason to resist his long-term temptation, especially because my romance with Louise blossomed. Louise wrote back to me along the lines of "very naughty to lie to her/ but brave to own up/yes, she'd like to see me again". Blimey! (as she always used to say).

Still unable to drive, as I really was only just 17, I trundled up to St Albans on the train to see Louise for the first time since Plas Newydd. It almost felt like we were starting again from fresh. This was a new timeframe – unrestricted days stretching out in front of us, instead of the safely confined Acorn week together; a new place – a tricky away fixture, featuring the 'meet the parents' moment; and a new age – what a plonker, putting myself at a disadvantage by pretending to be older. Sitting alone in the carriage on the way up, I felt a bit scared. I also remember thinking: "What if I don't like her?" But I did. And, while it hadn't occurred to me seriously to doubt it, she liked me too. The fact that I had an artificial leg was also completely irrelevant to her.

Left to right: Dave, Gillie and Louise, 1976

The first serious romance was really sweet. We wrote lots of letters and spent hours on the phone. She was mildly asthmatic and had a laugh like a hyena, but I wrote hilarious love songs for her such as 'Asthma-spray', closely based on the Beatles's 'Yesterday', in honour of her inhaler. This nearly caused her to have a fit in a St. Albans bus shelter, but we laughed about it later. I also wrote a soppy love poem about daffodils in Aberdovey, where they had a holiday house. St. Albans seemed a long way away, but I missed her even more when she was in Wales. I poetically enquired whether the daffodils were also blooming for her and whether "the paper moon, sellotaped to the window," was shining as brightly for her. Apparently they were.

As well as for saying "Blimey!" she was famed for wearing a red anorak with a big pocket at the front. Fond of fluffy wallabies, she called this pocket her 'pouch'. My parents had started a tradition of encouraging the children to paint doors inside the house. I lovingly immortalised Louise by painting my lady in red on the bathroom door in Dean. I knew I could not do justice to her sweet face, and I wasn't any good at hands either, so I painted the figure of her from the back with her hands in the famous pocket. So that people would know that it was her, I gave her the speech bubble saying: "Blimey, my pouch!"

My parents were remarkably tolerant of what my sister and I painted on their doors. Actually, Joanna painted two rather tasteful sea/harbour scenes. Sadly I became the victim of fascist censorship, or at least that's how I saw it at the time. When the vicar called round to the house, he expressed concern that the young lady in red was exclaiming, with a mild blasphemy, that her bladder was so full that she had to clutch it while racing to the toilet in the bathroom. My parents were mortified. I'm sure I might have talked the vicar round if I'd been there but, next time I went to Dean, Louise's speech bubble had been blanked out. And this was with a full 8 years to go before Orwell's authoritarian vision of '1984'. The other door censorship I suffered was more understandable. On the bathroom door in Hampstead, the room where we all cleaned our teeth, I painted a toothbrush. So far so good. However, the toothbrush was pink, with blue vein-like strips on it, and black bristles looking like pubic hair. And the tube of toothpaste was oozing suspicious white fluid. I blame Hugh Black-Hawkins. Actually, ALL of this is still on my dad's guest bathroom door. The only bit of my subtle phallic imagery that they did paint out was the purple knob on the end of the toothbrush. I only sulked for a couple of weeks.

I was very interested in playing toothbrushes and toothpaste with Louise. But, despite us both being at times soggy with emotion, we were put off by our inexperience, our conservatism and her bloody mother. Nevertheless I adored her and spent long hours dreamily looking at her photograph, especially when I should have been revising for A Levels. I even kept a log of when I thought of her during my A Level exams. The idea was that I would clock it and then get on with the writing but, as the five bar gates started to fill the page, it was little wonder that the grades were lower. "You'll be writing so hard you won't be able to w*nk for a week!" exclaimed Hugh Black-Hawkins cheerfully before one English exam. But I really don't think that in the end I did write hard enough.

Disabled Driving

Many of us were sent from school to a Camden driver-training centre in Mornington Crescent. Four of us at a time watched the same driving film and sat on 'stimulators' (actually simulators). These were crude machines that registered whether you would have changed gear correctly, stalled or over-steered as you went along. The moment I mentioned my metal leg, they set my car to 'automatic' and all I was allowed to do was steer. I was sorry to miss the early chance to practice the co-ordination of clutch and gear-stick when changing gear and the stimulator was a thorough misnomer as I spent a rather tedious time metaphorically staring out of the imaginary car window at my mates.

The first motorised thing I ever drove was my cousin's tractor round and round his field. I remember trembling with shock and being rather tearful when I eventually pushed the stop button, but the steering, the speed and the sheer momentum had been so exciting.

My mother, who had not long learned to drive herself, encouraged me to try a car with proper gears and took me on my first go in a real car. We took our old green Mini to a country road and I gingerly squeezed it into movement along the flat, straight road and then cheerfully reversed it back up again – fantastic! The pedals in a car are well positioned for me. To have the left ankle to squeeze the clutch feels like a more subtle movement than the right foot on the brake or accelerator, although smooth acceleration is also an art. My mother continued to encourage me and allowed me to drive to school every morning to practise.

The third gear on the old Mini used to pop out when you took your foot off the accelerator, which made cornering a bit dodgy and I couldn't take my test in it. I edged round the Winchmore Hill driving test course with my even edgier dad in his new Citroen. There was a moment of light relief when we spotted Wade Hill and I think I got a bonus point from the examiner for good road observation when I pretended to spot it for the first time during the test. So I passed my driving test at 17 after only four driving lessons. The examiner was fully aware of my disability and made a special check to ensure that he could award a full driving licence without restrictions. This has been incredibly helpful for hassle-free car hire and insurance ever since.

Naturally, one of the first places I drove to was up the A1 to St. Albans to see Louise. Nick was with me too and we were on the way to a barn dance at Louise's school. Like me, the Mini was more used to local school runs and the temperature gauge began to show 'trouble', with the radiator running dry. We pulled in at a garage and borrowed a watering can. We found the filler cap and poured a gallon of water... into the oil sump. Louise's dad took the mickey all weekend and it was a good lesson to learn, if only about Louise's dad.

The Prefect Pupil

I think it is fair to say that I was fairly pro-establishment in my later years at William Ellis School. I had been treated in an adult way by several of the teachers. I responded by respecting their authority and by doing my bit to help them uphold it (apart from the mooing in the Latin lessons).

My experience was that the school alternated in whether the dominant influence in each year was pro-academic or anti-academic, pro-establishment or anti-establishment. I was a pro in an anti year and this led to some difficult times in terms of peer pressure. I was never in a gang who got up to mischief. I think I was too worried about being told off to break any rules that were worth breaking. Thanks to being mates with Nick, I did manage to infiltrate the group who played with a punctured football in our socks on Hampstead Heath when we might have been studying in the sixth form. But when they melted away to have a cup of tea and a smoke in the local San Siro café, I used to let the side down by preferring to get excited by reading a book of Metaphysical Poets. I can still remember the exhilarating moment the penny dropped, when I discovered I actually understood what they were on about.

I was really too straight for my peers' tastes and I remember them complaining when I clearly wasn't inhaling when I took and passed on the joint in the prefects' study; knowledgeable 5th Years would sniff appreciatively as they went along the corridor. I strongly fancied someone from the girls' school opposite, but she shouted at me for accepting a cigarette from her (to try to look cool) and then letting it burn down without smoking it (because I didn't want to die prematurely from lung cancer, did I?). To appear to be trying in class was a real social no-no and it didn't help my motivation to study. I remember getting very good at rolling my biro to the very top of my textbook without it falling off, but it did take absolutely hours of practice when I might otherwise have been revising.

The school repaid me for supporting the establishment by giving me official status *in* the establishment. I was one of the first few in my year to be made prefect, I was appointed Vice-Head Boy and sent to represent William Ellis at St Paul's Cathedral for the Queen's Silver Jubilee service.

Being made prefect felt like a great honour at the time, it felt like recognition of me being a 'force for good'. In reality it meant having the honour to guard the back doors of the school during rainy lunchtimes, trying to stop cheeky youngsters from sneaking in against the rules. When I had championed the school rules for a year or so, it was time to elect the next Head Boy. It was clear to me that I was the obvious choice: a natural born articulate leader, never had a detention and

William Ellis School prefects 1977
I am 3rd from left, front row, next to headmaster Russell Perry

kept more cheeky youngsters out of school than anyone else. The snag was that there was some nod to democracy in the school, where the prefects were empowered to elect the head boy themselves from within their ranks. Popular winner was... a snidey, pretentious, pot-smoking boy from the heart of the anti-establishment crowd. Jealous? Me? The staff nipped in and rigged the election to make me and Dave both Vice-Head-Boy. I was mortified, and not just because sister Joanna had been runaway Head Girl at her school. Once I came to terms with my disappointment, I quite enjoyed the idea of being head of vice, although to be honest I was achingly short of certain vices for my liking. And the school, in some gesture of apology for the failings of democracy, snubbed the snidey, pretentious, pot-smoking one to send me, Harry Wade, to represent us at the Queen's Silver Jubilee service at St. Paul's Cathedral. Quite right too, I thought.

I drove the ancient family Mini to the official car park in old Smithfields Market and parked it deliberately in between two Rolls Royces. In my dry-cleaned school blazer I was very excited by the occasion and particularly taken with Princess Anne's canary yellow suit and Shredded Wheat hair as she passed within spitting distance down the central aisle.

It is curious to look back at these times and recognise the young man with a fervent and unquestioning belief in authority for the sake of authority. I now believe in leadership when it is good leadership and have a very sceptical view of authority that cannot justify itself, or listen, or change. We must always challenge the "Do not throw stones at this notice" brigade. But I had almost left William Ellis School before I learned to question authority.

The arc of my love affair with girlfriend Louise was suitably and symmetrically shown 12 months after Plas Newydd. Almost to the day, we drove together to Croft Castle for another Acorn Camp. The work was duller, the leadership poor and inconsistent. We spent every day battling with overgrown trailing rose bushes, which we described as "one sucker looking for another", for a grumbling leader who became known as Concrete Knickers. We met a big cuddly bloke named Teddy and his mate Andy (who wanted to be Ian Paice, the drummer from Deep Purple). Teddy was a lovely bloke. He was clever, funny and daringly anti-establishment. We had in-depth conversations about how he was questioning his Catholic faith as we stuck geranium petals for nipples on the naked ornamental nymph. Teddy walked on the grass mostly because the officious sign said that he shouldn't. Louise was adamant that we should walk on the path. I suddenly saw that I had a new choice and that it all looked more interesting than Louise. I was frustrated by our 'inexperience', I was frustrated by our 'conservatism' and I hated her mother (which was mutual), so we broke up.

Finishing School

So I finished William Ellis with a very academically modest record (see also convenient theories of dysgraphia in chapter Sitting on my Right Hand below) but I was psychologically very confident in me and my opinions. The re-marking of my English 'A level' was still not very helpful, I took the entrance exams but did not get an interview for Cambridge and I considered re-sitting my exams.

I was also very happy and relaxed to talk my way into Exeter University. After the first tricky question: "How did you get on in the re-sit?" "Er, I didn't", I really enjoyed a lively discussion on what I'd read recently. The sum total of this in the last 3 months was *Heart of Darkness* (102 pages), but it was fun to muse on whether English novels always featured going *up*river (in a colonial fashion) or downriver in American novels (discuss). Lots of panache and style compensating for any lack of hard facts. My future secured for the next three years, it was time to take a year off, get a job and go travelling.

MIND THE GAP YEAR

MY FIRST EXPERIENCE of paid work had been a Saturday job in Lindy's Patisserie. I was great with the customer relations but poor at tying knots. This became critical when a posh woman ordered a box of six cream cakes in a hurry, having parked outside on a yellow line. Cakes in the box? – no problem – but threading and tying the compulsory fiddly ribbon around the box was hard with my clumsy, unbending fingers. Without thinking I flipped the box over and the cream cakes all splatted onto the inside of the lid. The manager took over the heated customer and for my year off I resolved to look for a job that didn't mean coming home every night with fresh cream up my sleeves and in my pockets.

Brought To Book At The Local Public Library

From January to May 1978 I worked in Camden's Heath Branch Library. I borrowed books from it as a child and this is still my dad's local library in Keats Grove, Hampstead. The actual tree (*"or one very like it"*) under which Keats wrote *Ode to a Nightingale* stands outside. Although it is in such a relatively privileged area, and so less of a social and political priority, the very large numbers of Hampstead celebrities that live near the library have been very active and instrumental in fighting its closure over the years.

I have never been a voracious reader, although I read well once I get going. My mother would join in the game of trying to "guess which page I'm on", always guessing low to make the actual number seem more encouraging. I used to borrow Large Print books from Heath Branch because this made progress through the pages even more spectacular. I had just graduated to borrowing *The Joy of Sex* (for my Biology homework, honest! No, really!) which was embarrassing enough, slipped in with a pile of novels that I didn't really want, when I ended up joining the staff. Library staff get to know quite a lot about their readers. Full names, addresses and questionable reading habits are just a start. Libraries may have been quieter in those days, but there was still a chance to strike up a conversation and maybe a relationship with the staff. This reminds me of the story of a man who joined his local library and received his card from the attractive librarian. "So this means that I can take a book out whenever I want?" he asked. "Yes" she said. "And can I take out music and DVDs?" he continued. "Yes" she said. "And am I able to take you out?" he persisted. "No", she snapped, "Librarians are for reference only!" I guarantee there will be librarians all over the place howling at this one.

On a similar theme, one of the major plusses of me getting a job at Heath Branch Library was the chance to work with the pretty library assistant, who I had recently found out was called Bernadette. Already I had cut out renewing *The Joy of Sex*, to avoid looking too desperate, and I was timing my run so that she would be at the desk to issue my books. Calamity then to discover that it was she that I was replacing on the staff, and that she was going to America, and that she was marrying an American. Damn and blast!

Little did I know that this temporary job, to earn money to travel abroad, was to set up my employment off and on for the next eleven years. It is curious to think that my entire career path to date was prompted by a crush on a library assistant. The career path's sustainability was partly thanks to one new Heath Branch colleague, Nora Publicover, going on to be in charge of personnel for Camden Libraries. She would welcome me back from university for summer jobs, on one leg or on two, and later for a more substantive stretch as a graduate.

Working at Heath Branch was great fun. I could walk to work in 10 minutes and I didn't mind working every other Saturday when it gave you a whole Wednesday off instead. The place was full of characters, on both sides of the counter. Notable colleagues included Sue, Michael and Eileen. Sue had the most formidably efficient 'shelving' technique. Shelving is the bane of library assistants lives, putting back the returned stock and straightening and sorting the books. Sue was a well-oiled machine, rapidly pulling back each handful of books, lining them up in her palm and slapping them back on the shelf with a bang. In the time it took me to cover one bay, Sue had covered a whole wall. One should always respect expertise in whatever field, I think. Michael was a terrible shelver. He absolutely could not be bothered. Michael was an American poet (definitely not the American that Bernadette was going to marry). His poetry was obscure, much too dense for me, and too dense for most others as well, judging by the fact that he had to work at Heath Branch to make ends meet. Michael was surly with most customers ('readers') when placed 'on the counter', apart from the reasonable trickle of local literary figures that used the library. Michael would become animated, almost jocular, when Al Alvarez and others would come in. Otherwise he would mostly be found (or heard) in the side room, putting plastic covers on the new vinyl records we had bought and singing at the top of his voice to Bob Dylan on the record player. Eileen K_____ was more of the Sue model than the Michael. She was very efficient and always immaculately turned out. She had immaculate hair, immaculate lipstick and immaculate painted nails. She even left immaculate notes to everyone, in green ink, signed EK. So famous were the notes that she became known by her initials EK. No one had ever caught a whiff of gossip of any man in EK's life, so it surprised us all when she announced one morning that she was pregnant. We were of course delighted for her, and finally deduced that EK must stand for Emmaculate Konception.

My other notable colleague at Heath Branch Library was Linda and we are still in touch 30 years later. One of the main reasons for this success is because, despite my raging teenage hormones, Linda taught me how to be friends with the opposite sex without sex rearing its ugly head to ruin the friendship. We did promise each other that, if neither of us were married by the time we hit 30, we would marry each other. But we were, so we didn't.

The readers included the traditional collection of the eccentric, the smelly and the cantankerous. We had a strict rota for whose turn it was to deal with them. We discovered that only the ruthlessly efficient Sue could placate one particular reader, who was constantly complaining about everything to do with Camden Council, including the library service. Clearly she exuded competency that somehow calmed him from his rage.

Unfortunately, we also had sporadic visits from a woman whom I found very scary. She wore European clothes but with a full hijab veil that meant one could not see any of her face. In this quiet, tranquil environment she would burst through the door and noisily grab one of the public newspapers. Sometimes she would sit quietly for a while but then start to talk loudly to herself and begin to shout or scream before sweeping out of the room. I realise that this is not very high on the list of anti-social behaviours possible in a library but I developed a real phobia about her and my scalp would tingle whenever she appeared. I suppose I feared violence but probably the worst thing she would have done was to shout at me and it partly shows what a sheltered life I had led up to that time.

I was rather sad to leave Heath Branch Library when it was time for me to go off on my travels. Rather than go back to Lindy's Patisserie for my leaving cake I decided to cook my own. My mother made beautiful chocolate sponges and I used her hand-written recipe from her book. I'm not sure now why the sponge recipe had milk in at all, but anyway I misread ¼ pint for ¾ pint. I'm surprised that the mixture stayed in the tin at all, but I'm not surprised that it didn't rise much. I remember the branch librarian asking if I had used gelatine in the recipe, because of the unusual texture, but as good supportive colleagues they all had a small piece when I brought it in on my last day.

I Like To Be In America

I am a serial alarmist at airports. My metal leg always sets off the alarms prompting a good frisk from the security staff. I feel slightly cheated (and a little unsafe) when some staff take my word for the artificial leg and don't search me properly – who else are they letting through without checking fully?

The very first time I set off the alarms was also the first flight I had taken alone. I flew to Bordeaux on a French exchange as a 16 year-old and I was still in view of my anxious parents as the security guards pounced. To me it was all a great adventure. What better incentive to improve my French than pretty French twins quizzing me in the schoolyard? The French school was on strike (en greve) and we sat happily under a tree as they explained that (like my English) my French was rather formal and old fashioned. I got rather stroppy when a boy demanded if I approved of power for the people, because I wasn't really into left wing politics, until the twins explained that he was merely asking if I liked Deep Purple.

Loaded with all the money earned at Heath Branch Library in my year off I flew out on my tour of the USA. Long before the terrorist attacks of 9/11, I still met a very jumpy (and heavily armed) policeman at JFK airport. As usual I'd set off the flashing lights and he seemed to be sweating as he told me menacingly: "OK, buddy, back up there, easy does it". Luckily metal legs still don't seem to count as potential weapons, unlike tweezers, or else I'd probably get it confiscated on the plane. At least this would double the legroom.

I travelled to America with Max, whom I'd known from William Ellis since I was twelve. I wouldn't say that we were particularly close at school. Max was in my small Ancient Greek group and he scored 106% in his Maths exam – it was deemed so difficult that they marked the 'percent' out of 110. I can't remember how much social engineering our parents did to get us together, but in many ways he was an ideal person to travel with. He was tall, wiry and pale and enjoyed the lonesome, contemplative art of cross-country running. We fell out over his lack of decision-making and that every time he got a nosebleed he insisted on going for a run, but his greatest asset was his aunt. Max's aunt married a Texan called Manning with seven brothers dotted round the country – mercifully not all in Texas. We were therefore able to plot our course based on either somewhere we were particularly keen to go or else where one of the Mannings lived. We ended up covering 12,000 miles on a Greyhound bus, passing through 39 states in about 2½ months. My leg held up quite well but my bottom got rather sore; it eventually returned to its normal shape but it was an awful long time to be sitting down.

We arrived in a heat wave and spent the first few days acclimatising with some friends in Princeton. We slept in, had the mind-expanding combination of bacon and maple syrup pancakes for breakfast and tried to get to grips with the technical data of baseball on TV – just what were RBI's anyway? The new extreme temperatures were difficult for me because of sweaty stump socks. We caught a bus up to New York City and trudged around the central area rather than commit ourselves to the scary subway system. We went up the Empire State Building and skirted the Statue of Liberty on the Staten Island Ferry. We had a couple of half-contacts in New York that we over-optimistically thought would put us up for the night. We trudged several more blocks to ring these apartment doorbells, but the trail ran cold as my leg was running rather hot. Blistered and bothered we beat a retreat back to Princeton. We'd learned a lesson about forward planning and the following day was the first of several that holiday that I spent unable to wear my leg while the blisters healed.

Next stop Philadelphia. We viewed the Liberty Bell and began to realise how the American story of the War of Independence was going to have a distinctly different slant to the one we had learned in school. Another new lesson came in Phili bus station. At the top of the escalator stood two shady characters who offered us drugs. This had never happened to us before (apart from in William Ellis School prefects' study) and we found the experience unnerving. Two months later we once more changed buses in Philadelphia on the home leg of our journey. At the top of the escalator stood the same two dudes offering their wares. This was now small beer and we just walked on by.

There is no doubt that we both grew in confidence and worldly wisdom thanks to our American adventure, although I was not exactly short of self-confidence in some areas already. Indeed a little more modesty may have been in order, judging by the diary I kept on the trip. I should have been more gracious to our various hosts, who often put themselves out to meet us from the bus station. They were very generous with their hospitality, especially considering that, apart from Max's aunt, we were not related to any of them. It sounds like I was rather dismissive of one host's attempt at a new phonetic English dictionary, once he revealed that 'hot' and 'heart' were in the same place as far as he was concerned. And I certainly should have been quicker to cash some travellers' cheques to buy the beers with one family who were short of a few dollars.

However I most wish that I had been more assertive with one of the many Texas Mannings who had laid on the welcome barbecue for the English cousins. They lived in a cul-de-sac circle of houses in a suburb of San Antonio. The community basketball hoop was in the middle and they had invited in Dan the neighbour because he wanted to ask if I knew his grandmother in Luton (I didn't). All was going well with the big all-American welcome until Dan's son Jim trotted up.

There was a problem because another boy had thrown Jim's football back to him when it bounced his way. It was a problem because the other boy was Mexican. The local view was explained apologetically that "some idiot" had sold one of the houses to a Mexican family. Dan reassured Jim that if the other boy touched his football again he would get a baseball bat and smash his brains out. The party all cheered, but it left Max and me feeling queasy. The casual but menacing racial divide was very shocking. The following day we went down to another Manning in Corpus Christi, on the Gulf of Mexico (as if we hadn't just experienced the gulf in San Antonio). Here the hospitality was again very generous but today's more painful problem was that I was stung on the stump by a jellyfish when swimming in the sea. A jellyfish sting is never pleasant, but the red wealds that came up made wearing my leg very uncomfortable.

Waynesville, NC, where the one horse had just left town

Early highlights of our tour included the poshest gents toilet I've ever been in at the Chatanooga Choo-choo and the most amazing one-horse town called Waynesville. Waynesville consisted of one main street that looked like a two-dimensional Hollywood set for a cowboy film. All the facilities appeared to be called Bill's Bar and Bill's Taxis and Bill's Store. We asked an old boy, wearing the full Stetson and chequered shirt, if Bill was some big local business mogul. When he eventually understood what we were on about he laughed his head off, as this had never occurred to him before. We got back on the bus and headed for New Orleans.

New Orleans before the Hurricane of 2006 had already become quite an edgy, dangerous place to be. But in 1978 it felt a very relaxed city with the fabulous southern belle architecture. For two dollars we sat on the floor in the smoky, poky Preservation Hall, transfixed for a couple of hours by the most amazing jazz. It was played by three really ancient black men and their substitute trombonist, a white man who may have been a mere 55. This would compete for a place in my 'top twenty things I'm glad I did in my life'. The sheer skill and panache of the band was extraordinary, a live performance like this never to be recaptured.

Declining my first ever chat up line from another man, we headed west out of New Orleans and into Texas. It is very easy to get into Texas by bus, but takes *days* to get out. I used to take my leg off on the longer trips overnight. Leaving the leg lying there was quite effective in discouraging people joining the bus from sitting down next to me. It was a real asset, and a blatant goal, to get two seats to yourself to stretch out to sleep. However one fellow traveller did sit down and suggested that I 'put it in the footlocker', which made us both laugh. With many hours to kill on the bus out of Texas we got chatting with other fellow travellers. They too were on their way to Flagstaff to go to the Grand Canyon. After some negotiation, two Englishmen, two Dutchmen and a Norwegian ended up hiring a fat convertible car together and driving the East rim of the Canyon. In 1978 the East rim was hardly developed at all. With our own transport we could hang around until all the coach tours had headed home. The colours of the sunset on the red canyon walls were indescribably beautiful. There is a part of me that is content that my camera had already packed up by then. Although I was very upset when my slide film returned from the processors with blank after blank, some of nature's greatest natural beauties are better captured and stored in the memory rather than an electronic device. On reflection I believe that this is true too for the man-made beauty of events such as the live jazz from New Orleans. The red earth glow of the deserted grand canyon at sunset will stay with me forever.

Also glowing, though rather less edifying, was the fascinating array of false teeth in the glass cabinets along the main street of Juarez. Some cross the Mexican border to seek a new life and some to seek new teeth. They also do a good line in second-hand artificial legs, although of course a new second hand might have been even more attractive to me. We actually crossed the border to look for very cheap tequila and came back clutching a massive bottle of warm, ready-mixed Margherita. We sipped it on the evening Greyhound as it pulled out of El Paso, goggling at the temperature display reading 112 degrees. Too damn hot!

We did casinos in Las Vegas (the cheap, bus station end, where the free breakfasts were the major draw) and Disneyland in LA and Max had a nosebleed and so went for a run underneath the Golden Gate Bridge in San Francisco. I got offered a scholarship to a minor college in Oregon on the grounds that I was taller than the basketball coach who was on the same lumber mill tour as we were. Finally we arrived in Seattle, to be met by Max's aunt, the indirect source of so much accommodation. We crashed there for a few days, grateful not to be on the move and particularly not to be on the bus. My lasting memory of our travels with his aunt was the delicious chicken stew she cooked for us that, during the meal, was revealed to be in fact one of the family's pet rabbits. My daughter Katherine endured a similar "oh-my-word-tricked-fluffy-bunny-equals-delicious-food" moment in Turkey, which she fronted up bravely in the face of provocative banter from her brothers.

Leaving Max with his aunt in Seattle for a few days I travelled further north into Canada. In Vancouver I had a most emotional reunion with Mrs Elisabeth Hurt, one of my teachers from New End Primary School. I had hardly had any contact with her for twelve years, but we shared a very genuine and instinctive warmth that is hard to explain. I was eight years old when she had been my teacher. She and her husband came for dinner with my parents on more than one occasion, which I was daringly allowed to stay up late for. I can see how a small boy would idolise his teacher, especially one as kind and gentle as her, but I can't quite figure out to what extent she had a special connection with me as a child that could make the transition into adulthood. I got to know several of the teachers at William Ellis outside of school (not just cheap labour to lay Mr Hickman's patio and to paint Mr Black-Hawkins's kitchen, surely?) and which continued as a friendship later in life. Despite our original age difference it felt entirely natural to me to greet Elisabeth on equal terms. I stayed with her and husband and her children taught me how to skateboard down the drive at the back of the house. This was a big improvement on the only other time I had stepped on a skateboard. I had chosen wrongly by putting my artificial foot on the board and pushing off with my left. No ankle means no balance and I was temporarily horizontal in the air, about a metre off the ground, before plunging back to earth as the skateboard scooted off alone down the hallway.

I spent my 19th birthday in Vancouver. Max arrived to join the celebrations and because it was also shared with Canada's Dominion Day we had quite a party. I met up with some Canadian students who I had helped to guide round London when still at school. Why they should want to see me again I shall never know, after I was mainly responsible for taking them to watch Arsenal draw 0-0 with Stoke City and dragged them round the royal carriages collection in Victoria in the pouring rain.

We learned a lot on our American tour, not least how to read the ferociously complex Greyhound Bus schedules. We came to understand how to perfect the art of connecting buses and therefore minimise the time spent in grotty bus stations. The individual plastic seats with the individual coin-operated TVs, like the nearby McDonalds, were to be avoided if possible once the novelty wore off.

Our greatest finesse with the Greyhound timetables came after one of our greater cock-ups. We were heading from Vancouver to Denver, via Calgary and Salt Lake City. This is a mere 1,700 miles or so, and we planned to tour by day and sleep on the bus by night. We were still sleeping off the Dominion Day hangover when we travelled over the Canadian Rockies into Calgary, so I remember little of their majesty from out of the bus window. However delays on the serpentine road meant we arrived in Calgary after the last bus that night had already gone south. We asked at tourist information about hotels, but they laughed at us. It was the weekend of the world-famous Calgary Stampede and all hotels for miles were full. Undeterred, we used Max's prodigious mathematical brain to work out the crossing point of the Greyhounds between Calgary and Vancouver. The critical success factor was the little town of Revelstoke. We slept for four hours up the mountain passes from Calgary, played Frisbee for twenty minutes at 2 a.m. in Revelstoke Main Street and then slept for three and a half hours downhill back into 'Cow town' just in time to catch the 06:20 south to Salt Lake City.

Donny Osmond was a big star, two or more wives still sounded like an attractive opportunity rather than an expensive legal obligation and we had been on the bus for a day and a half. We decided on a tour of Salt Lake City. At the back of the upper gallery of the magnificent Mormon Tabernacle we were suitably impressed that you actually could hear a pin drop down on stage. We also looked up our family names in the famous genealogy library. However we had heard that complying with the numerous requests to give our names and addresses led directly to an increase in doorstepping from young men in smart suits with great teeth but who were not called Donny Osmond. Accordingly we assumed the name of George Davies on every form we filled in. At that time, this man's name was plastered all over walls in the UK suggesting that he was a victim of an injustice. Max and I reasoned that if anyone challenged our identity in Salt Lake City we would simply assert that George Davies was innocent.

Our final Manning lived in Denver, where gas-masked demonstrators were protesting about the city's promotion to the USA's second most polluted city. These Texans out of Texas had a holiday home up in the mountains in Cripple Creek (which caused some jokes at my expense from our hosts). The altitude gave Max a nosebleed, so he went for another run, only to find it hard to catch his breath for the same reason. I was more concerned by how hard it was to boil a kettle at altitude for a cup of tea.

After Denver, it was the long haul home across the middle of the middle of the USA. It was a shade over another 1700 miles in a straight line, so we broke our journey in Kansas City and Cincinnati. In Kansas we stayed with Paul, my American Cub Scout friend from nine years previously. Paul's family took us to see some live baseball, where the Kansas City Royals excitingly won 10-1. We had spent the last couple of months studying the baseball on a range of televisions from bus station to bar to beach house in Santa Barbara. Max now drooled excitedly over the extreme mass of statistics that baseball delights in (including RBIs of course) whereas I was more taken with the computer co-ordinated fountains that spurted every time anything interesting happened. They used a lot of water that day, particularly when someone finally whacked the ball out of the park. This was definitely NOT rounders played by men in pyjamas.

Bernadette, her three cats and Max in Cincinatti

Homeward bound, we travelled in our faithful Greyhound across the miles and miles of cornfields. The sun began to rise in a golden glow over the USA's breadbasket. As we continued the journey the land became more hilly and the sun was lost behind them until it rose again in another golden glow. Bigger hills, lost the sun again, rose again, golden glow #3 – slightly weird experience... Cincinnati meant Bernadette, the much admired library assistant, and her recently acquired American husband.

Bernie's husband was a medical student who took some photos of me for his professional interest in my very unusually shaped stump with a unique Bill Clintonesque kink in it. To follow this theme a little further, we began to realise as he snapped away that the stump, rising from between my 'real' leg and the metal one I had slipped off, looked extra large and lewd.

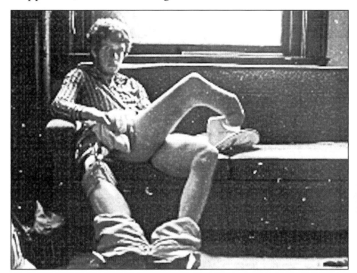

'The medical model'

It was good to see Bernie again, but they were both at work all day and we were dog tired and looking homeward. So we did not stay long, but climbed back on the bus for the final leg. We brushed past those drug dealers at the top of the escalator in Phili Bus station; we counted the number of passengers in the throng waiting for the New York bus to calculate whether there was enough to make Greyhound fulfil its promise of putting on a second bus if the first one was full; and we draped ourselves expertly over two seats for that final snooze before we checked in again at Princeton. Our Princeton friends the Browns (son Chris had been at New End with me for a year) kindly drove us to JFK for the flight home.

On the way to the airport Mrs Brown broke to me the news from home about the death of the old family dog Bracken. Bracken, a White West Highland, had been a Pink West Highland when we bought her. The runt of the litter, she had been out in the rain and had been beaten with a copy of *The Financial Times*. Unlike most of her breed, Bracken was a coward. We have home movie footage of her backing away from an over-friendly lamb and she regularly bolted home from walks on the Heath if alarmed.

Bracken, the White West Highland, with her half of Teddy

Bracken was both a coward and a counsellor. Often was the time I remember as a teenager sitting at the foot of the stairs hugging the dog and telling her earnestly that she was "the only one that understands me". She was a good listener and I was the one that was barking. Otherwise, her main party piece was to shut the door. The television at home was in a position where, when the dog came padding into the sitting room, the door would swing round and block the view. After some training, at the command of "Shut the door!" Bracken would jump up to the door and slam it shut. Perfect for the armchair sports fan. But the sad news I received in the USA meant that we'd have to shut the door ourselves from now on.

I'm a complete convert to the idea that "travel broadens the mind". I learned a lot from my American trip about self-sufficiency and self-confidence. I met with triumph and disaster, surviving the sleazy pool halls of Birmingham in Alabama and the squidgy handshake of Pluto in Disneyland and treated those two impostors just the same. My mind still required a good deal of broadening, but I returned to England much more of a man, and not just because I was sporting the fledgling beard that has barely left my chin since.

Flying Fifteens And Gay Gordons

I spent the remaining summer months of my year off mooching around London. As a welcome diversion I headed for Ilkley in the Yorkshire Dales to stay with my cousin Andrew in his beautiful house with his beautiful wife and their beautiful four daughters. We played tennis on the beautiful grass court that he had grown himself. There was a distinct home advantage when we played, knowing the patch of moss on one side of the service box that made the ball shoot through in a completely unplayable way. I would wear their mother's old wedding hat to amuse the young cousins and we played "bad eggs" incessantly, which involved throwing the ball up in the air and then running like mad to hide in the rhododendron bushes.

Andrew had a boat on Windermere and occasionally he would invite me sailing when we visited and we even entered a race or two. I had little to offer in terms of sailing skills other than good eyesight to spot the marker buoys to head for. Andrew's Flying Fifteen didn't get out much and probably didn't have the pristine polished bottom enjoyed by the boats of the elite of the Royal Windermere Yacht Club. Our best finish was 4th, but another time we were overtaken on the long home straight by four boats. As we sailed in to moor outside the RWYC posh clubhouse, a disgruntled Andrew barked at me to grab the pontoon as we slid past. He then changed his mind and decided to do one more circle for a better position. Sadly I was already anchored more to the pontoon than I was to the boat, and after a brief impression of the Clifton Suspension Bridge I slid gently into the water up to my chest. My hollow metal leg filled up with water (quick! A seat for Dr J____) and the RWYC members cackled over their G&Ts as I clambered out of the water. They went a bit quiet when the pump action of the leg's socket made water squirt sideways out of the ventilation holes with every stride, like a mini fountain at Versailles.

I won't dance – don't ask me! My earliest dance movements as a toddler, as recorded earlier, were to nod my head in time to the music. 47 years later this remains, according to my wife Mary, my most attractive form of dancing. I was so unconfident at school discos thinking, as I still do, that I look like John Cleese doing his silly walks. But I never danced more than in my year off, when I was practically a season ticket holder at Cecil Sharp House – the headquarters of the English Folk Dance Society.

The lack of an ankle is a disadvantage to a career in ballroom dancing and terminal to one in ballet. This has not been a long-term regret for me. I was however delighted when a new type of artificial foot (the Seattle sash) allowed me to hop for the first time on my right leg. I could still be someone in the Morris Dancing world! (and put my trousers on my left leg without having to sit down...). The resilience and bounce in this moulded plastic sash foot meant I could skip for the first time – this is now appreciated more by my daughter than by my sons. I regularly used to attend the Saturday night ceilidhs at Cecil Sharp House in Camden Town.

Unlike school discos, where you can only touch the girl in the last dance, folk dancing involves a lot of holding hands and other physical contact throughout the evening. It involves quite a lot of swapping partners, so that you have a good chance of ending up dancing with a prettier girl than you had the courage to ask to dance in the first place. For a young man it has an attractive feature of the short-term achievable goals of getting some complicated moves 'right' (i.e. you all end up where you started) although many young men are now more fulfilled in this by computer games. You can be cheeky, daring and fun by not just taking eight steps but by charging as far away as you can within eight beats and then hurtling back to perform the next bit of the dance (how we laughed). But most of all you can be manly – in a chivalrous way. You can hurl your partner around in a 'basket' – where the two men link arms behind the women's backs, plant their right feet in the middle and scoot with the left to spin the women off their feet. Actually, an artificial leg is really useful for this manoeuvre because it is very easy to spin and pivot with an ankle that won't turn and a foot that doesn't mind being trodden on. You can hurl your partner – and everyone else's partner – around in 'stripping the willow', my personal favourite; and you can most extremely hurl your partner around by spinning with her in the final frenzied polka. I was lucky enough to be hurling a statuesque girl called Lucy in one such polka at Cecil Sharp House when the very strict laws of gravity and centrifugal force got the better of us and we landed in a heap. Hooray! It was several years later, when I had a ceilidh with local band Hips and Haws as my 21st birthday party, that my Morris dancing chum Will Benson revealed that the basic moves with the hankies are simply miming two balls and a cock. Cissy they are not ...

I did dance on the table at last year's works Christmas do (it was a dance-on-the-table themed restaurant). I have a reasonably musical ear but, perhaps because I am so tall and it is a long way from my ear to my feet, I am not convinced that my disco dancing is very rhythmical, let alone cool. It has been suggested that the punk era should have been my moment, where a suitable adaptation of my metal leg would have made me a pogo-ing king. But the most fun I have had dancing in public was at the over-sixties disco I organised for Rag Week at Exeter. We bussed into the university a hundred pensioners from the clubs around the city and I organised a fleet of friends with cars to ferry the stragglers. We rock and rolled together in the student union for several hours, with Sid and Ada twisting their way to the floor and having to be pulled upright again. Of course I enjoyed slow-dancing at the Summer Prom with the mouth-watering Karen to the Korgis's *Everybody Gotta Learn Sometime*, but you can't beat an old-folks' rock and roll for sheer enjoyment.

When we were young, my sister once borrowed my spare leg to go to a fancy dress party as Jake the Peg. This was a 'loveable' character created by Rolf Harris in the late Sixties. Joanna cut a hole in the pocket of my dad's old mac and swung the leg around to copy the comic three-legged dance that went with the act. The accompanying song was along the lines of:

> "I'm Jake the Peg . . . With the extra leg
> Wherever I go, in rain or snow,
> The people always let me know:
> "There's Jake the Peg . . . With the extra leg.

Hilarious and harmless fun, of course, although it's interesting how it captures the inevitability of people making a sideshow of someone with an odd number of legs. This is not worth a rant.

A middle leg was also required when I was trying to learn to salsa. We fondly remembered Jake the Peg when trying to step off the middle leg, partly to move away from lewder associations.

A footnote to the dancing, if I can call it that, is a memory of a boy named Barry doing *The TV Times Tingle*. I met Barry at Roehampton, where he was being fitted for both legs, below the knee, like mine. *The TV Times Tingle* was a dance from a 1960s advert that involved vigorous high kicking and running on the spot. Barry performed it brilliantly on his stumps in the waiting room. And yet he was the boy that had been told by the 'specialists' that he was disabled. He was sent to a 'special' school and did not think he could ride a bike or climb ladders, whereas in fact he could. It was a curious and cruel study of conditioned disability. I'm different – I'm just not very good at dancing.

THE GRADUATE
EXETER UNIVERSITY 1978-1981

UNIVERSITY! A NEW HOME! A new life! A chance to be a completely new person! These were the thoughts I no doubt shared with the vast majority of students arriving at university from generations before and after. I was utterly certain of my total originality, like all those before and after me, while I just continued to grow slowly out of the old person.

Technically I was there to study English literature although I spent a lot more of my time enjoying the Music department rather than the English one. I was carrying the flag for Hugh Black-Hawkins, but my strengths with literature have always been to dig deeply rather than widely. "Suck! Suck!" cried Hugh in our English lessons. I could drain a Hardy poem dry or hoover up a DH Lawrence short story. But in James Joyce's weighty Ulysses I never really got past the toilet scene at the beginning, including the kidneys' heady aroma with a whiff of urine. I certainly never got as far as the famous monologue at the end, despite the promise of sexual content.

I did dutifully attend Shakespeare at The Northcott Theatre on the university campus. Highlights included *Macbeth* on a minimalist stage. Lady M sat alone on a single chair, reading of her man's promotion to Thane of Cawdor. Lights dim on single chair and go up on the balcony at the back where Duncan is arriving. Duncan surveys the scene and announces: "This castle has a pleasant seat". Good spot, Duncan, as there was certainly nothing else to see... (cue inappropriate laughter from student audience). *Hamlet* in modern dress was the next play in the series. Lounge suits for all the courtiers. Once the king had enquired sneeringly: "You told us of some suit; what is't, Laertes?" (cue inappropriate laughter from student audience) I decided to stop attending Shakespeare at The Northcott.

I managed to wangle a single room in my first year at Mardon Hall. The Hall president supported my bid not to share a room, like most first years, on the grounds of my artificial leg: suggesting that a room-mate might fall over it when staggering in late at night. Mardon was still an all-male hall in 1978 and the communal shower rooms proved to be a dangerous place for me. Confident and strong on my left leg, I hopped out of the shower onto the lino, but my foot slipped and I banged my head in a heavy fall. The shock made me queasy and I have treated showers with more respect since. Sometimes hopping has to be attempted if the cubicle is too narrow to crawl into and then stand up; picking up the soap from the floor of the shower is related to this, as is washing your standing foot. I was discussing the necessary bending-down width for a new shower recently with my plumber, who claimed that he never actually washed his foot but assumed the falling water would do the trick. This is an attractive excuse not to bother with the "unpleasant bending", but I also promised my old 'leg fitter' Jack Cosnett that if he looked after the artificial one I would look after the fleshy one and that includes preventing athlete's foot. 'Level or favourable access to a shower' does not seem to be covered by building regulations or the Disability Discrimination Act. Even posh hotels with sumptuous bathrooms still have showers that I have to crawl into and use sitting down or would take ropes and crampons to climb up to.

My three main Mardon mates were Gareth and Bill (who did share a room) and Derek. Gareth and Derek were from Warrington and Widnes respectively. I met Gareth on my very first day. I found him excitingly non-conformist, in a non-religious way, and he had a whiff of being mad, bad and dangerous to know. For a start, he listened to Gentle Giant and Genesis (just listen to those almost criminal bass lines and rapid changes in the time signatures). Gareth and I fell out over a girl, but we resolved it in the traditional Mardon manner. This meant duelling

Up on the roof of Mardon Hall, 1979. Left to right: Derek, me, Keith and Gareth

with soda siphons in the corridor. This was sanctioned, and even encouraged, by the Mardon hierarchy, with the siphons being supplied by the hall bar. Gareth and I embraced in a manly way after charging up and down the corridor jousting with the squirting soda. This method only failed to resolve disputes between Mardon members if someone used the siphon for hitting rather than squirting. Derek struggled particularly with how posh everyone was at Exeter. At first we ribbed him mercilessly for his funny northern accent, but he was resilient and quick-witted enough to shrug it off and we eventually forgot about it. He even tried to defend us to his brother's mates, who were all Widnes firemen, only to be ribbed mercilessly as a southern softie himself. He now lives in East Grinstead.

I spent my first independent New Year's Eve in 1978/9 with Derek and Gareth in Warrington – my first real hangover and the only time I've ever beaten up someone else's snowman. A year or two later the snowman's curse was returned. It has been the only time I've ever been beaten up, while on a pub crawl with Derek in Norwich, although some express surprise that it hasn't happened more often. Usually I have been successful in talking my way out of trouble rather than into it.

You will get the theme of various drunken escapades that are apparently reinvented every year by each new wave of first year students. I can confess on these pages, for the first time ever in public, that I was the man that unscrewed the last screw on the mirror on the top landing in Lopes Hall and then watched in horror as it fell and smashed. While I'm at it, I may as well get off my chest that I also volleyed the strawberry yoghurt against the wall on Mardon staircase and dangled the bag of lime jelly outside the warden's window. I can assure you that all these events seemed hilarious at the time.

First Night Performance

Also officially hilarious was the Mummers' play that I cobbled together in rhyming couplets for Exeter Rag Week. The fact that it was Europhobic and slightly smutty made it perfect material to perform from a hired cart in the cathedral square. Gareth, Derek and Bill were all participants along with a large flagon of scrumpy and we may or may not have raised a laugh, let alone money for charity (none of the above can remember this sort of detail – mainly due to the scrumpy).

The most unexpected and amazing outcome of this artistic effort was that we picked up, in pop star terms, a groupie. The bountiful young lady in the red beret advanced from taking part in the audience participation, to taking me back to my room, to taking off my clothes, to taking my cherry.

This is perhaps a suitable time to reflect on going to bed with an artificial leg. I take my leg off when I go to bed. It's like you might take your shoes off: more comfortable, not a clunky, hard presence in the bed. I usually take the leg off with the shoe, sock, trousers and pants still attached – NB pants and left sock to be changed in the morning. If the fire alarm goes off, on balance it's usually worth pausing to put the leg on rather than hopping down the fire escape. You get a number of 'bonus' clothes on in the same movement, which puts you one up on the poor souls standing naked in the car park.

Occasionally this routine backfires. One morning I was wearing clean underwear with the clean-enough trousers left on the leg from the previous day. I had taken the train to London and was striding down the platform at St Pancras. My left ankle was slapped by a piece of cloth that had caught round my plastic foot. On inspection I realised that yesterday's underpants, which had been hiding overnight down my trouser leg, had worked their way undetected down the leg and were now flapping round my ankle. In one smooth movement I swooped down and effortlessly tucked them into my jacket pocket, pretending that I had just dropped my handkerchief.

On another angle of going to bed, taking all these bits of clothing off in one movement is a fabulous short cut when heading for bed in the height and heat of passion. However there is an issue around taking your leg off with a girl you don't know very well. How much do you tell them beforehand? Do you stash the leg under the bed and wait for their toes to find out that they outnumber yours 2 to 1? Will the explanatory lecture on prosthetics dampen their ardour, scare them off completely, or excite them because if they have a good imagination it looks a bit like a large penis anyway? Ok, this has never to my knowledge actually happened, but there is something appealing about the shorter leg. As a little boy I used to beat it on the carpet in the style of Bambi's friend Thumper, and my sister named the leg "Sweetie" (not the rest of her brother, mind). It is smooth, rarely being exposed to the elements, and was favourably compared to the muzzle of a gundog – but I can't really tell you any more. Having two legs is more stable than one leg, wherever you are. But wearing the leg can cause unintentional (and sometimes unrealised) injuries, although there are less sharp edges than there used to be. And there is always a fear that one is missing out on some tender footsie footsie because they are stroking your leg and the vibrations are not quite strong enough. "Knock three times on the *sealing* if you want me" was surely the song Tony Orlando & Dawn meant in their mega hit in the 1970s?

Back in Mardon Hall, that Summer the first time, a quick calculation of the above leg-removal options ended in me deciding that I would take it off, with a quick warning for my partner about the tripping hazard.

Conversely, I once triumphantly kept a girl out of bed by taking my leg off at night. I was late arriving at a party where many people were staying over and all the beds had been reserved, so I put my sleeping bag on the floor. I went to bed before the person who had put her stuff on this bed, so I playfully slipped my empty leg under the end of her duvet, sticking out a foot at the bottom. A little later she stumbled into the room and wailed: "oh no, there's someone in the bed already, the swine!" (or thereabouts) and went off to find another bed. It seemed a terrible waste to leave the bed empty for the night, so I slipped under the duvet and slept a treat.

When there is love, the disability is irrelevant. The tangle of legs in bed doesn't matter if it contains three or four. Four legs good, three legs better?

Physical touching and cuddling has always been very important to me. My mother was a very good cuddler and we used to have a family song and dance routine called "Four little dollies in a tub, tub, tub" where my mother and father would hold us all close and dance in a circle. On reflection this sounds very similar to the Cecil Sharp 'basket', which may be why it appealed so much. I love to cuddle the ones I love, and I feel cut off without it.

I don't think I got extra cuddles by having a car at Exeter. Exeter University has always had a tradition for a group of super-rich students called Wellies. They were responsible for us topping the university league for students with TWO cars, so merely having the one was relatively unremarkable. However, to be able to offer lifts did get me welcome extra company at times. My mother didn't do the clenching of fists and hissing "Yessss!" but she reported doing her own milder version of it when I returned home that first Christmas with a glamorous blonde in the passenger seat. In fact it was only Debbie who, although she evidently was a glamorous blonde, on this occasion was just a mate cadging a lift most of the way back home to St Albans. Debbie and I became mates through Caroline Harris-Reed, who was also beautiful, witty, rich and far too much fun to risk mucking it up with clumsy romantic notions. I can't now remember why I entered Caroline's room on my knees. Several of my mates were there in those early university days when people congregated in large groups while the friendships shook themselves out like a wet dog. It all went a bit quiet when Debbie exclaimed: "Ah, here comes the cripple!" I skewered her on the point of her embarrassment for a little while, with a series of running gags (that was probably one of them) about her putting her foot in it (that was another) and not toeing the line (...) and shopping at Body Shop. You get the picture. I don't suppose she used that phrase again, and we also became good friends.

A girl called Sandy accepted a lift to Ottery St Mary where, if you pick the right day, the locals carry barrels of flaming tar on their backs until it burns them. We held hands in the dark, on the way back to the car, and it emerged that she had a quicker dirtier mind than I did. I was rather taken with her, if a little overawed, but I got the message that we were to 'become good friends' – rather than anything else – when I called on her and found her in bed with one of Mardon's Welsh rugby players.

Sarah accepted a lift to East Coker. This *must* have been early on in my first year, because I was still enthusiastic about English literature and one of the students who studied it with me (i.e. Sarah). Both of these faded rapidly and by years two and three Eng Lit had become a rather annoying distraction from enjoying my time in and around Exeter. East Coker is yet another reference to TS Eliot, being the name of one of his *Four Quartets*. Sarah and I dutifully walked in the "deep lane shuttered with branches, dark in the afternoon, where you lean against a bank while a van passes". Sarah came across as quite straight and a bit plummy, much like the girls from Mrs Kellaway's class that I had been used to at William Ellis. I was therefore a bit shocked, and surprisingly attracted to her when, having seen the generations of the Pollock family commemorated in East Coker church, she wrote "Too many Pollocks" in the visitors' book. I acknowledge that this may seem anti-social and probably offensive to anyone connected to East Coker church or the Pollock family. However I have always been drawn to that whiff of challenging naughtiness: the Teddy and the Gareth. Like a good book, I will always value the first sedition.

Despite her daringness in the church visitors' book, Sarah found my passion a little forward and we went our separate ways (probably because I "came a bit too close" – another bit of *East Coker*). My frustration, bordering on desperation would have to wait a bit longer until the Mummers girl gave me the release papers from being a Mama's boy. I therefore considered it a badge of honour to contract glandular fever – or the 'kissing disease'. That said, I was very lucky to get it only mildly. I had had a sore throat for a day or so when, walking up one of the hills on campus, I suddenly had the need to lie down on the grass. I struggled back over the hill to Mardon and lay wiped out in bed for a couple of days. My throat was so swollen that I could not eat solids and my cousin called by with the bowl of lime jelly that eventually ended up swinging outside the warden's window. I was sent home, but made such a rapid recovery that, after a couple of days, I was out and about again. I took the opportunity to go to see my old William Ellis friends playing a gig in Dingwalls at Camden Lock in a band with the very appropriate name of Sore Throat.

Mardon Hall was lots of fun and perfect for the new friends frenzy of the first year at Uni. I started the Exeter University Mah Jongg club, which met in Mardon every week and brought welcome funds to the hall bar. I'd learned to play at William Ellis and still enjoy 'twittering the sparrows' which is the imaginative name given to the sound of the decorated bamboo and ivory tiles being clacked together. The students union eventually gave me a grant to buy some sets and the toy shops of Exeter scrambled to get some in as we toured round them making enquiries. The reluctance of the students union to fund the Mah Jongg society stemmed from an officer with a long memory. He reported that the authorities had been forced to close down the previous version after the gambling element of Mah Jongg had got out of control. Rumours of Triad involvement had surfaced after members' rooms had been broken into to pay gambling debts. I assured them that our version of the club was more like gin rummy with a few extra winds and dragons.

Dressed up for the First Year Rep's Disco at Mardon Hall, 1979

Back at full energy I was elected First Year Rep. I don't recall attending any Mardon committees, so my main task was to organise the First Year Rep's Disco. We decided to make it fancy dress. At least Derek, Gareth and I definitely wore fancy dress and were (therefore) hilarious. I did find a magnificent trouser suit at the Alphington Ladies' Conservative Association jumble sale. It was mostly fluorescent pink, with diamond patterns of yellow, lime green and blue. What is it that makes students, and particularly male students, want to dress in this way? Is it "the male's emergence from his drab camouflage into the gaudy plumage that is the birthright of his sex"? (*Hair*, 1969) Or is it a collective lack of judgement that mean that none of the males have the nous to spot that, instead of looking hilarious, they actually look a prat? I think Gareth actually wore the A.L.C.A. trouser suit on the night, while I wore a pink bit of curtain with a blue hem, an Anderson tartan cap and a string of tinsel round my neck. My lasting impression of the night was watching a wild lusty woman from Barnstaple express herself energetically to the song *(Ooh) Black Betty (blam balang)* but, unsurprisingly, she didn't express herself very near me.

Finally, having a car actually meant escape from Mardon Hall and the chance to live a more grown-up life out in the Devon countryside. While Gareth, Derek, Bill and I all had a custom made "We all like sheep" t-shirt (loosely adapted from Handel's *Messiah*) only Bill and I had a car. One minute we were all going to be back in Mardon for another year and the next minute a house in the country came up and we were gone. I had even applied to be Hall President, and there were dark murmurings from the hall faithful about the first ever *external* candidate and my lack of commitment. One of Caroline's connections had heard of a place that had just become available and so Bill and I moved into Brown's Farm, Splatford for the next two years.

Duets on the lawn at Splatford with Bill Benson on trombone

A QUICK TRIM

AT THE AGE OF 20 it was time to lose the rest of the foot bone. It was originally left to give a better, longer stump for the metal leg to fit round for a very small boy learning to walk. Now it had grown quite long, at a backward angle of 45 degrees. This gave my right leg an odd bulge at the back as the metal legs had to grow at the back to accommodate it and I ended up looking like I had a supremely developed right calf, like I cycled a lot but only used my right leg to pedal.

I became a bit of a draw for visiting medical students at Roehampton because of the interesting shape of my stump. This series of pictures were given me by a student who was part of the crowd that had gathered to watch the complex process of making a cast for a new socket to go inside the metal leg. You can see I was wearing my best bottle-green Y-fronts as I sat on the chair protected by a paper and plastic sheet. There was little room for modesty as the star attraction.

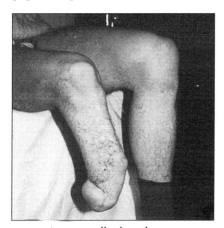

An unusually-shaped stump

The metal strip to protect from the Stanley knife

Because of the bulge at the end of the leg they had to cut off the cast once it had been made. For this reason the first stage was to bend a metal strip round the stump to run up the side of the leg. How we laughed as Jack would later stick the

Stanley knife into the setting plaster of Paris hoping that the metal bit was still where he left it.

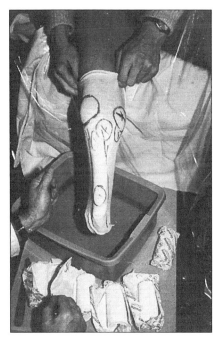

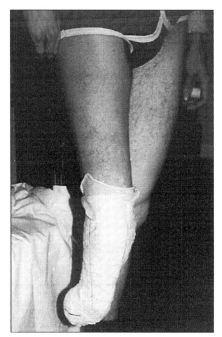

The wet cotton sock with the purple dye pencil

The finished plaster cast

While the metal strip was cold, it was swiftly followed by a warm, damp sock. On the sock Jack would use a purple dye-pencil to draw a relief map of my most exciting contours. This transferred to the cast to give the socket-makers a clue about where to leave extra room for the pressure points. Then came the strange sensuality of the plastering process. Dipped in warm water and eased onto my sensitive stump, smoothed onto the curves of my knee and the long shin bone, the bandages built a faithful model of my lower leg.

Jack would make sure to pinch a little around the metal strip so that when it was time to whip out the knife there was at least plenty to aim at. Once the plaster had begun to set the cast was cut off and the cold damp sock was discarded. The purple dye would stay on my leg for several days, looking a little like a set of mystical tattoos or a pirate's treasure chart as I sat in the bath.

The odd shaped stump did not help my balance, but more importantly the unprotected bone rubbed terribly during exercise. At Exeter I would choose to play squash knowing I would then need to hobble or hop the following day, just as a hot day of sightseeing in the USA would preferably see the next day without my leg on. I have also kept the woollen sock with four bright orange darning mends that someone's auntie in Vancouver performed to keep me mobile. The wear and tear was becoming serious.

I had a new choice now, but a difficult one. We agreed with the doctors and fitters at Roehampton that I had probably stopped growing and therefore I could have an operation to trim the bone to make a better-shaped stump. The shin part of my leg was long enough for me to lose the foot and heel part. The long-term gains of having a regular shaped stump should outweigh the short-term inconvenience and risk of an operation.

I had the op at Queen Mary's Hospital Roehampton, on the same site as the limb-fitting centre. I was allocated a bed in the LSU, the Limb Surgical Unit, not La Sainte Union Convent School opposite my old school where I'd been hopeful but hopeless at getting a bed for years. The side rooms each had pairs of beds and I was put in with Paul. Paul was a 17 year-old punk who had lost a leg in a motorbike accident. He played me basement tapes of Adam and the Ants – quite daring at the time – and was visited by hordes of mates who rattled their chains and squeaked their leather around the ward. Paul had a birthday while we were both there and even Rosie, the 90 yr-old diabetic, gelled her hair up for the occasion.

Roehampton, near Wimbledon, is a long way from Hampstead across London. My mum came nearly every day and she sponsored (bribed?) my mates Nick and John £5 "to cover bus fares". Nick brought a melon, which we ended up playing football with, and John accompanied me to the ultrasound clinic, where we played "ohmygodsomething'sgonehorriblywrongit'soutofcontrol". All John's older siblings had baby-sat for Joanna and me in the past but John and I are much the same age. John was a late, and possibly 'unexpected', blessing for his parents and so had been previously deprived of the ready income from The Wades enjoyed by the others for lightweight care of me. This at last was some compensation. We've been best friends ever since, I would trust him with my life and everything except my Chelsea memorabilia (a Spurs fan), so it was £5 well spent.

I was in Queen Mary's Hospital for three weeks, a week extra because of an infection, and it surprised me how hospitalisation is a condition that affects the mind as much as the digestive system. I sulked when they gave me the weaker white pain killers instead of the pink ones, was very sad when one day no-one came to visit me at all and over-excited when a nurse offered to wash my hair (although that's probably fairly normal).

I even wrote teenage angst poetry:

Wednesday's Child

On Wednesday I went back inside
I knew exactly what it would be like;
I knew the pressure on my psyche
From regimented well-defined tranquility,
And doubted my ability
To conform and smile while from within I cried.

This last July I played a game
Of tennis, on a Wednesday afternoon,
And hardly realised that soon,
In seven days, the dreadful tag "disabled"
Was mine: inexorably labelled;
And worse, compelled to live up to my name.

Inside I had my weeks of pain;
We were physically and mentally degraded,
And little now has passed or faded.
"Back with us once more?" remarked the nurse,
The same as ever and yet worse,
When on Wednesday I went back inside again

There were some very low moments that summer as I contemplated disability at a much deeper level than I ever had before. An essay I had to write for Exeter was about Wilfred Owen and I got quite upset and obsessed with his (rather better) poem simply called *Disabled*. It is about a sporting hero who "threw away his knees" in the war.

Now, he will spend a few sick years in institutes,
And do what things the rules consider wise,
And take whatever pity they may dole.
To-night he noticed how the women's eyes
Passed from him to the strong men that were whole.
How cold and late it is! Why don't they come
And put him into bed? Why don't they come?

The expression by Owen of the anger and the bitterness has rarely been my experience, but the fear of 'sick years in institutes' suddenly felt more real and you will recognise my dismay at potentially losing 'the women's eyes' over to 'strong men that were whole'. The essay I wrote was far too long and complicated; it scored poor marks from my tutor, but I found it very cathartic to write.

Back in Roehampton, the staff nurse, Kate Beverley, was fantastic at trying to keep up morale and was complicit in The Great Escape over the wall. By the third week I was getting stir crazy in the hospital so John and Nick engineered a trip to the pub. Kate found us a wheelchair, as I hadn't a leg to wear, and she agreed to leave the fire exit open. It was downhill to the pub and we played police motorcycle display teams with John and Nick doing balletic things on the wheel chair's back bars. We had a few pints and it was high time to get me back to the institution. There was far less enthusiasm for pushing me back up the hill, I remember, but we hit a problem when the side gate was locked and it was miles back via the main entrance. I don't remember it very clearly but I do know that the wheelchair and I both made it over the high hospital wall in one piece and I let myself in through the fire exit as the lads scampered off after the late bus.

It was a ward of two halves. One half of the ward was for amputations to legs that had been healthy and the person was to go on to learn to walk again with a prosthetic; the other half were the diabetics with chronic circulation problems. For the latter half, in single bedded side rooms, the doctors seemed to have to cut and cut again, and sometimes (like gelled-up Rosie) they died when there was nothing left to cut. Given this contrast of conditions for the patients, the staff were magnificent in their care for all of us. They put me with Paul because I was a good example of positive life on one leg and, far from getting morose, we mostly had plenty of laughs. It is also true and probably important to say that my leg *bloody hurt* that summer! I don't pretend to understand how a limb repairs itself when a bit has been cut off. How do the little capillaries mend to make the circulation work properly again? The industrial grade painkillers were essential to stop the piercing shooting pains that snagged up my body from the leg. For years afterwards I would consciously compare my memory of this sensation with any pain experienced elsewhere. Pain is totally relative, and the dentist became a breeze compared to the post-op throb.

Hopalong Harry

Just as I became ready to walk again after my operation, the leg-makers walked out and went on strike. It left me without a leg to stand on and so I went back to work at my summer job with Camden Libraries on one leg with crutches. I could sit on a stool and issue books; I could staff the enquiry desk, although if anyone wanted me to show them the section on Australian marsupials I was reluctant to hop over to show them; and I was relieved from the big book-shelving chore, because that really is tricky on one leg.

The lads were on strike for three weeks. This led to some nasty blisters on my hands from the crutches. I conducted my own sociology survey about how many people actually offer you a seat on the London Underground when you hop onto a crowded train, or how miserable or stroppy do you have to get before their conscience gets the better of them. The answers are of course: a) 'precious few' and b) 'very'.

Later that month I was caught trying to break out of a nurses' home on one leg. My old school friend Raj had somehow perfected his 'mojo' so that women found him irresistible. His specialist subject was nurses. I got to tag along to chat to the random friend of Raj's latest stunning conquest. On this occasion we were back in the University College Hospital nurses' home in Gower Street after a night out. It was 'after hours' by the time I left and the extra nurse went back to her room, leaving Raj to spend the night there. I took the lift to the ground floor but I found the main doors were locked. I didn't know the geography of the nurses' home well enough to know if there was a side entrance, so I clanked around on my metal crutches looking for it. Eventually I encountered a senior nurse and politely asked her if she could show me the way out. Unfortunately she became inquisitive about why I was there at this hour. Rather than give away my friend Raj and get his partner into trouble, I made up a story about having fallen asleep, but not being able to remember the number of the room or the name of the person in whose company I had fallen asleep. I admit that this does not sound very convincing. I assumed that this sort of thing happened all the time in nurses' homes, although I may have seen too much of 'Carry on Doctor' (i.e. all of it). I assumed the senior nurse would say: "Well you've probably been a very naughty boy, I'll have to give you a warning and if matron were here she'd probably give you one too". And we'd all laugh at the anticipated double entendre and then call it a night. Unfortunately she called the police. I had to come clean and I was frogmarched, if this is possible on one leg, back up to the girl's bedroom where she put her head round the door to confirm that she knew me and then I was allowed to go home.

It still seemed unlikely to me that a man intent on attacking someone else would attempt it on one leg; apart from anything else you needed both hands to hang on to the crutches and, in the event of trouble you would have to 'do a hopper' rather than a 'runner'. On the other hand I have newspaper clippings about a man who had his artificial leg confiscated by a judge because he used it to beat his wife, and another who had his leg stolen by thieves just so that he couldn't chase after them. Raj eventually got rumbled when my parents fielded a phone call from his worried parents at 2 a.m. I'd been back at Exeter for weeks but he was still telling them that he was out with me when in fact he was playing doctors and nurses elsewhere.

The long summer vacation dragged by. I was missing my new friends from Exeter and, really and truly only having one leg, meant that I couldn't go and visit them (although I was a 'shoe-in' for my first orange disabled parking badge from Camden Council). Caroline came with Debbie to visit me at home and she drove me to Kenwood House. The flowerbeds were fantastic, but I felt a bit of a chump having to stick to the flat paths on my crutches.

With Caroline Harris-Reed at Kenwood House, 1979

Later in the summer Caroline had a big birthday party at her parents' posh house in Great Missenden. Still unable to drive on one leg, I had to persuade an Exeter acquaintance called Viv to drive me out there. The printed invitations for Caroline's party said: "Dress up" on them. I quizzed her carefully what this meant, but she said airily: "It means whatever you think it means". Well "dress up" to me meant "trouser suit from the Alphington Ladies' Conservative Association jumble sale" – my turn to wear it this time – and I persuaded Viv to wear the pink and blue curtain thing. I assured her we'd look hilarious. When we got there I banged on the door and swung in on my crutches in a blur of fluorescent pink. Everyone else was wearing evening dress. I don't think Viv spoke to me again after that night, although it probably didn't help that I got drunk and tried to persuade her, alone by Caroline's swimming pool, to leave her long-term boyfriend and come away with me.

Over the years I have had plenty of practice on one leg that brings skills for all readers to try at home – or not. For instance hopping upstairs with a cup of tea – try water for starters. Picking things off the floor takes some practice, as does urinating accurately into a toilet without a fatal wobble due to loss of balance. Then again, lowering yourself to sit down on a cheap toilet seat can be risky. I have demonstrated that the momentum of a big man sitting down on a flimsy toilet seat with only a slight sideways angle from one leg can end up with both on the bathroom floor.

On Top Of The Pylon

Once the leg began to heal from the operation, the swelling went down and the leg-makers at Roehampton came back to work, I was given a temporary leg or 'pylon'. Because of the swelling, when the stump is changing shape so rapidly, there is no point in having a made-to-measure leg until it has settled down. The name pylon is apt as it looked like an electricity pylon, with a loose-fitting fibreglass bucket, two rods of metal and a slab of wood bolted on the end, but to me it was a limousine to fill the flapping trouser leg. With several layers of extra woollen socks, I could put a bit of weight on it to take the strain off the standing foot occasionally, and it helped to reduce the stump to optimum shape for the new-style lightweight leg. I still needed the crutches to get around.

The pylon was not, sadly, terribly stable. It was held on by a small leather strap over my knee that couldn't be pulled too tight because it stopped the knee bending. The result was the occasional mishap. I was waiting for a tube at Camden Town. When it arrived, I swung into the carriage but caught my trailing pylon on the step. This caused my leg to slip off down my trouser leg and it was left standing freely on the platform as I landed in the train. I dropped the crutches and luckily I was able to hop off the train and scoop up my leg before the doors closed. The passengers looked rather dumbfounded and sat there open-mouthed, but I reassured them: "Don't worry, this happens all the time". Bucking the trend of my recent survey, I was actually offered a seat by a middle-aged white male.

So my pylon was perfect as a temporary fix for some limited mobility to get around, and it was also perfect for water-skiing without troubling Dr J_____'s blood pressure. I dusted off my pylon the following summer when I tried water-skiing on Lake Windermere.

Waterskiing on Lake Windermere – so little wind resistance

It had many advantages for this, as it was light and very streamlined. It had virtually no water-resistance for getting up on to the surface and no wind resistance for slowing you down. The romantic image is complete of me, in my rubber suit, ploughing a furrow across the still lake with the wind whistling through my *leg* (rather than my hair). There are two further advantages of the pylon for water skiing. These are that when you fall over and the leg falls off it doesn't a) fill up with water (see sailing, above) or b) sink. In fact the wooden slab of a foot bobs quickly up to the surface and acts as a handy marker buoy for the boat to pick you up.

After the trim operation I had physiotherapy and learned to walk with a completely new type of plastic leg that made my real knee do a lot more work than it was used to with the old metal hinges. Two of the most radical changes were the loss of the thigh corset altogether, just the little leather strap above the knee, to stop the leg slipping off, and a conversion below the knee to a more standard PTB, which means Patella Tendon Bearing. The principle is that the socket squeezes the stump just under the knee to take the weight. The moulded socket was a rigid but squishy plastic. It absorbed some of the pressure of the knee sitting in it. There is quite a lot of movement in the knee joint and the socket has to have just the right amounts of pressure in some places and clearance in others to prevent serious blisters. This is a precision business, because when the skin won't heal in this load-bearing place, you can't wear your leg at all.

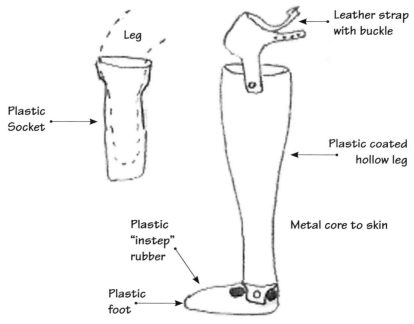

Leg

Leather strap with buckle

Plastic Socket

Plastic coated hollow leg

Plastic "instep" rubber

Metal core to skin

Plastic foot

The presentation of the rest of the leg was also a revolution for a teenager in that now it was foam rubber covered in a pink plastic skin. No more cracking of hard boiled eggs on this one and no more danger signals, or injury, for anyone accidentally knocking against it; from a metal shell to a soft, slinky and squeezable version. I felt altogether more squeezable myself. The foot was a great improvement too. It was solid plastic that flexed and an ankle that rocked (like me on the disco floor – well potentially anyway).

The resistance to the forward rock was called the 'instep rubber', a very hard slab of plastic slotted into the foot to help the spring in your step. Time and again this proved the weak link in the outfit as I pulverised them in quick succession, particularly playing sport. The forward lunge in badminton to clear your opponent's drop shot must have done for boxfuls of instep rubbers in my time. When the instep rubber gives way the leg develops a sag to the front. This spoils posture and walking position and leads to blisters because the weight shifts, so I had to drop by my local limb-fitting centre to get a new rubber. For some this is a major expedition that takes all day. But luckily for me, London, Exeter, Sheffield, Cambridge and now Leicester, all the cities I have either lived, worked or studied in, have had hospitals with limb-fitting centres. The current name they use is Disablement Services Centre. The pit stop at the body shop for a new instep rubber could mean as little as a couple of hours off work on a good day.

While the instep rubber was physically weak, the small leather knee strap gave me some psychologically difficult moments. Maybe linked to the pylon problem on the London Underground, I was sometimes worried it would fall off under pressure. I had a close shave on a fairground ride on Hampstead Heath called Paratrooper. People often lose shoes as you are whirled round and high into the air. I could feel the leg slipping as the centrifugal forces got to work and I quickly crossed my legs to prevent it flying off and therefore me kicking someone to death from 50 meters away.

The BBC featured a man going through the process of learning to walk again after losing a leg in the 7/11 bombings in London. Natasha Kaplinsky was practically tearful at the wonder of this man walking with a plastic leg. I found this a little irritating, considering that it is a process that so many hundreds of people go through every day. To give him credit, the man was reasonably modest about his own achievements and properly praised the support staff. The process of adjusting to walk with an artificial leg is undoubtedly far, far harder that learning to walk with one from scratch as a toddler. One must have the psychological hurdle of trusting the technology at the same time as still working through the loss of the 'real' one. I have met many fellow patients, sitting through the long hours waiting for our legs to be fine-tuned during the fitting and repair process.

Some are understandably more bitter than others, especially those that have lost legs through an accident, but the modern materials and technology make trying on a new leg not a million miles away from trying on a new shoe.

The new plastic legs are so advanced compared to the old metal monsters. Roehampton had a gallery of glass cases with classic models from past decades. I've worn quite a few of them myself. One of them is the type that Douglas Bader wore when he was a Second World War flying ace. One of his legs sold at auction in 2008 for an amazing £115,000, although it is not known if this was one of the pair that the Germans guards took away from him because he kept escaping from the prisoner of war camp. I bet he would have found his way out of that nurses' home though.

THE MUSIC OF LURVE

MUSIC WAS THE central focus of my second and third years at Exeter University. I lived in Splatford with Bill Benson, who was studying music, and an increasing amount of my social life revolved around people from the orchestra. I was constantly on the horn.

The very first time I played the French horn was at a circus on Cup Final Day in 1968. On a rainy day at Chessington Zoo, we took refuge in the circus tent, where some clowns were trying to recruit children from the audience to play in the band. Never slow to volunteer, I was the only one who could get a noise out of the French horn. We marched around, everyone playing in their own key, and although I was only 9 years old it must have sowed a seed. I began to play the horn in earnest at William Ellis. It suited me well as a great left-handers' instrument, since the four keys are all pressed using the left hand, while the right hand is mainly just stuffed up the bell. I passed Grade 6 at school, without much enthusiasm. I would never practise during the week. The perk of having a heavy instrument is that I always got a lift to school. My mother said she wished I had taken up the piccolo. Sometimes this lift doubled up as my weekly practice session, where Mum would stop the Mini in a Hampstead Heath car park and block her ears while I blew the cobwebs out of the other end of the horn. I actually gave it up twice, in writing, but my inspirational music teacher, Richard Hickman, refused to accept my resignation.

At Exeter, with a new teacher, Brian Sampson of the Bournemouth Symphony Orchestra, a new Holton Double horn and a new range of beautiful, artistic girls to sit near, the University Orchestra provided an enlarged incentive to practise. For my first concert I had to borrow my father's dinner suit. He was at the time rather wider around the waist than I was, which meant I had to wear his maroon braces to keep the baggy trousers up (although this also meant that they bounced unnervingly up from the ankle as I walked). I distinctly heard Derek and Gareth shouting "Coco the Clown!" from the back of the gallery as I walked on stage. It was an unwitting tribute to the origins of my French horn playing and I suppose I should have been grateful for them coming to support me on my big night.

We had a very democratic horn section, meaning that everyone got to play the big tunes sometimes even if we weren't absolutely the best player. The pinnacle of my playing career was to be first horn in Tchaikovsky's *5th Symphony* in front of a packed university hall that included my parents. I played the famous horn solo at the start of the 2nd movement, which sounds a little like one of John Denver's greatest hits, and it has a nasty leap up to a high note that made me very nervous. My pitching of high notes was helped enormously by some clever occupational therapists at the local St Loyes College. They created a special glove out of leather that effectively extended my right hand to full width. Although the right hand is 'mainly just stuffed up the bell', an extended hand helps the airflow and makes the pitching of high notes more secure; they put a stiff panel in the glove alongside my fingers to effectively give me a couple of extra fingers. The cleverest bit of the glove was a small pocket of polystyrene balls that extended the fleshy palm of my hand. This allowed me to 'hand stop' the horn, which blocks the air and changes the note to a tinny parp. Some composers insist on it.

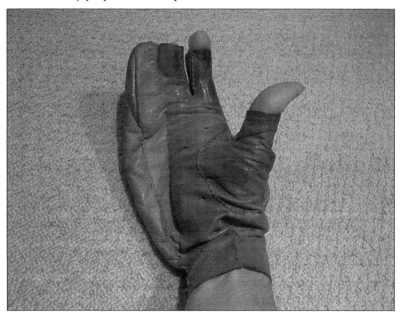

The French horn glove made for me by occupational therapists at St Loyes College, Exeter

Thanks to conductor David Cawthra's connections, and persistence, we were able to play with some international stars of classical music. This included Rachmaninov's 3rd Piano Concerto with John Lill; Tchaikovsky's *Violin Concerto* with Gyorgy Pauk and more Tchaikovsky: *Variations on a Rococo Theme* with brilliant young cellist Julian Lloyd-Webber. "Was JL-W good enough to get into the National Youth Orchestra?" asked my slightly naive cellist friend, another Caroline. This was the aspirational band for most decent school musicians but, while this achievement had been beyond Caroline (and me), I tried to explain to her that he had probably had bigger fish to fry. I must also give due mention to Caroline's exploits during a public performance of Berlioz's *Symphonie Fantastique*. During a frenzied passage for the cellos she lost her grip on her bow. Sitting on the outside desk there was nothing to stop the bow from sailing off the stage and landing on the wooden auditorium floor with a huge "clack!". Caroline's face was a picture of embarrassment and bewilderment as she gripped her now redundant cello. Happily, a young man from the audience came to her rescue by picking up the bow and returning it. Caroline's clack was preserved perfectly on tape as the concert was recorded, but sadly I lost my copy when my car was burgled. They were welcome to the Genesis and Dire Straits, but the Exeter concert recording was irreplaceable.

Splatford And Sarah

My second year at Exeter began with the preliminary Mardon week with the orchestra. It was funny going back into the hall knowing that I had so recently decided to leave it but this was where the university orchestra always had its week-long play through. There were incoming first years (although I had been too cowardly/modest to go in my first year) and we acquired two more very good horns to make it a strong line-up. We immediately got stuck into the horn quartets. Our lips were well developed by the week of constant playing and so we carried on playing an energetic quartet arrangement of the Hawaii-5-O theme tune past two o'clock in the morning until someone threw a pillow at us.

The arrangement of sharing Brown's Farm, Splatford with Bill worked very well. Unlike those tough northern boys, Derek and Gareth, Bill was a southern softie like me. He was much shorter than me with a good size nose and suprisingly blue/grey eyes that bulged alarmingly when he got excited. He had instinctive comedy slapstick timing and tears rolled from his eyes when he laughed. We both had early bum-fluff beards but he wore a cloth cap and smoked a pipe, even when he wasn't trying to be funny. His father was a doctor, who never saw 50% of Bill's holiday snaps because of the telltale pipe sticking out of his back pocket. Bill was a very unassuming man who developed a taste for very assuming women. Last time I saw him he was happily married to a very well-organised woman, with seven children between them.

I can't remember a serious row we had over the two years we lived together. We were both reasonably domesticated, although I think he was a more experienced and better cook than I was. I reprised my famous Heath Branch library chocolate cake, this time with the correct proportions and better results, but Bill seemed capable of using the oil-powered Rayburn that we had in the kitchen to make casseroles and other exotic dishes. Keeping the Rayburn burning was the only rule that our farmer's wife landlady insisted on. We were very self-contained with our own front door and even a little garden. It felt like a little isolated cottage in an idyllic Devon valley. The sun would pour in over the rim of the landscape bowl we were in and fill it with warmth. One could forget from day to day that we were grafted on to the main farmhouse at the back until Mrs Boyle appeared through the magic connecting door to collect the rent from time to time. Having a secret parallel universe going on through an unused door on the landing was a bit like *The Lion, The Witch And The Wardrobe* – without the lion... or the witch really because Mrs Boyle was a very nice lady. The only time we ever fell out was when I tried to move the supplied MFI wardrobe to a different place in the bedroom. What had once been self-assembly rapidly became self-disassembly as bit by bit it fell apart in my hands. I felt like Buster Keaton at the end, surrounded by a collection of horizontal bits of imitation wood lying across the floor, but still clutching the handles of the two cupboard doors.

Low budget version of The Italian Job co-starring Bill Benson

Bill and I operated a low budget version of *The Italian Job*, having just the red and the blue minis between us. Every morning driving onto campus involved playing chicken with the postman coming the other way in the strictly single-track lanes. Who would brake first and reverse to the occasional passing place? Would anyone actually have time to brake at all if you met him on one of the really blind bends? Eventually the old red mini I had began to play up. My parents gave me permission to use it as part-exchange for a new one. This was the first time I had been involved in buying a new car and the salesman at the mini garage in Exeter did a thoroughly professional job on me. He offered me just £50 for the old car. I mean it wasn't that old and it was still a lovely runner (most of the time). Deflated, I put an advert in *The Express and Echo* for £75. The phone was still ringing nearly a week later for such a bargain and I probably could have sold it for several times that amount. Even then I naively allowed the old boy that bought it to con me into driving it out to his house near Exmoor and got Bill to fetch me. I have since cultivated the reluctant, doleful and cynical approach needed to get the car salesman to work a bit harder for his or her money.

I don't remember if there was a specific moment when Bill picked up the name "Splatford Wife" (perhaps after the *Stepford Wives*?). This referred exclusively to his domesticated role rather than any suggestion of reciprocal husbandry. He was a good friend, who earnestly assured me after I had seen Genesis in concert that they were a significant contribution to the evolution of modern music. I know others have used a similar but different word to 'contribution' to describe Phil Collins. Bill was also very tolerant when I started doing the thing that disrupts so many households: I brought a woman home. This was not Sarah M, who liked TS Elliot and I went to East Coker with, nor even Sarah W, who lived in Lopes the girls' hall and had a sexy neck; this was Sarah from Weymouth, who I met at a disco and was a trainee occupational therapist.

Many years later I have cause to reflect on the origin of the species, or at least its future prospects, when the selection processes are so suspect. Why, when I already knew so many females at Exeter, including all those already mentioned, whom I admired or loved more than Sarah, did I end up going out with the trainee occupational therapist from Weymouth? By the way, I think occupational therapists are fabulous! Was it really simply because she would have me? I fear it did us both few favours at all and, if she ever reads this, I feel I owe her some sort of apology.

Sarah was kind, sweet and eager, but her dad reminded me uneasily of earlier girlfriend Louise's. And while Gareth and Derek helped me to rechristen her home town "Wey-Hey-Mouth", the relationship was regrettable and quite quickly regretted. She asked me to shave off my slowly developing beard and I wasn't happy. She asked me to spend less time with Gareth and Derek, who confused her with one of the Werewolf Sisters. Eventually she asked me if I would rather that we were "just good friends." I jumped at the chance and enthusiastically agreed that this should be the case from now on. Even though this was officially her idea in the first place she seemed quite upset. When I reported the conversation to my "what women really mean" adviser Sandy (we genuinely were just good friends) I was told that apparently mine was a WRONG answer. I was supposed to say: "No, no, everything is peachy, I love you still". Suddenly, buying a new car seemed straightforward.

Beer, bolognese and bog roll with Bill Benson ... but no beard

What did remain straightforward was that Bill and I continued to enjoy each other's company, when we weren't getting distracted by women. Over Christmas 1979 I went to visit Bill at his home in Aylesbury. We had been asked by the university students' union to visit an Exeter student who was in nearby Stoke Manderville hospital. We were happy to help and I remembered my dark day at Roehampton when nobody at all came to visit me. But she seemed unimpressed by our chirpy banter and said rather accusingly that we had only come because we had been asked to (which was true, of course). Bill and I repaired to a nearby pub so that I could add it to my pub list for the year.

Every time I went to a new pub and drank at least a half pint I could add it to my 1979 pub catalogue. It was a very student thing to do, marking the pub out of ten for quality of the beer and overall impression. There was also space to make observations about the pub, usually a critique of the bar staff. The dangerous part of this slightly geeky but otherwise harmless pursuit is that it encouraged one to visit more pubs and also to drink and drive. I was on 187 different pubs for the year and I had already used up all of the local Hampstead ones. Could I find another 13 in the next 5 days to make it a round 200? So we had a half in the pub in Stoke Manderville and then several more as I racked up six more pubs in

Aylesbury. And then I had a coffee at Bill's house and drove home. Just outside Aylesbury I was stopped by the police. Crikey! I was dead meat. I switched off the cassette player, wound down the window and gave him my best Hampstead "Good evening officer!" The tone I was going for was lightly spoken, quietly respectful and stone cold sober. He asked me what was in the boot of the car. I avoided all the possibilities for witty repartee and told him that it was just the spare wheel and a foot pump. He stared into my eyes, but didn't ask me to get out of the car. He told me that there had been a few cars stolen in Aylesbury that night, and again I was non-committal and only moderately interested because he'd told me and he was a police officer, so he must know what he was talking about. "Well I won't keep you... have a safe journey home, sir". I was extremely lucky that night, and I haven't been drunk in charge of a car since.

Bill was particularly pleased that we became known at our local pub near Splatford, the Anchor in Kennford. He was tickled by the fact that the landlord would reach for two pints of Courage Best as soon as he saw us walk though the door. However this was the dawning of the age of video games machines in pubs. The Anchor installed one of the first Pac Man machines and I was consumed by the blue dots and more often by the four floating monsters. We called it 'Gobblers' and I quickly developed a major Gobblers' blister between my thumb and forefinger. This is where you have to grip tightly the knob on top of the steering lever to eat the dots and flee the monsters. Nearly thirty years on I still have the callous where the blister came and stayed for a while. What is worse, the assistant barman at the Anchor had the time and the access to work out the safe routes round the Gobblers maze so that I didn't even have the honour of the coveted High Score.

Eric And Emma

My final year at Exeter brought more music and I fell head over heels in love. Unfortunately these two things clashed slightly. We started with another wonderful orchestral overture week in Mardon. Another splendid new horn player in the shape of Andy and more horn quartets – even to the point of performing a concert in a local church, where we rather brashly called ourselves Bull By The Horns. We could all play loud at times, but Andy could play louder; and we could all hit high notes, but Andy could hit higher. Yet despite his talent, Andy was the opposite of brash, sometimes needing coaxing through when he wasn't fully sure what he was doing. We played a lively piece by Chabrier called Espana – which we knew as A Spanner. It suited well Andy's loud and high qualities, but he developed a mental block about some tricky triplets that he had as a solo. Practically the whole orchestra was bobbing up and down on their chairs to help him through while we played the regular rhythm around it.

Orchestral drag for Rag Week with 'Deaf Ed'

I was lucky enough to be one of the two horns in Exeter University Chamber Orchestra that year. We went out on the road to perform in other parts of Devon, and once to Exeter's twin city of Rennes. In Rennes we were billeted with French families, wined and dined at the Hotel de Ville and then we performed at the grand theatre opposite in the main square. We were not responsible for the fire that burned it down a week later. Domestically, we played a memorable concert in Bridport. There were only about six people in the audience and all were fairly elderly. One of the pieces we played was by a final-year music composition student called Tim. We were all given a series of notes that we had to play, but we could decide when and how fast we played them. This chaos resolved cleverly into a climax where the motifs finally came together and as players we rather enjoyed the piece. Sadly this was lost on the paying audience. We were encouraged to mix with them at the interval, partly to make them feel less lonely and probably partly to block their exits. "It sounded like we were in a madhouse!" one of them complained loudly. But we were able to tempt them back in for the second half with a promise of some soothing and accessible Haydn. I remember with such pleasure the buzz of a performance and the camaraderie of the band. We huddled in the coach, late at night, on the way back from a concert, with Sue the bassoonist wearing her Orchestral Manoeuvres in the Dark badge. We didn't like their music but we liked the idea.

Sue had returned to Exeter for her fourth year having spent the third year abroad as a language student. Many of her friends had therefore left after three years and so the orchestra was a good family to rejoin. We quickly became close. In a moment of inspiration I wrote *Eric the Rabbit* for her. In truth the moment lasted about three hours, or the train journey from Exeter to Paddington. It's the story, in rhymed couplets, about a rabbit who wins a crossword competition and goes to Spain, where his girlfriend Felicity the Frog has a spat with a matador. You know, usual stuff. It enjoyed a few minor edits once I got back to Exeter, and one or two bits seem a little dated now (like the reference to 'bead-strewn Bo Derek' – although it did rhyme with Eric) but it remains probably the best thing I've written. Apart from this autobiography of course.

Eric became quite well known among orchestra friends. But he really took off when a clever music student called Graham undertook to write some musical accompaniment. Graham's music, written for wind quintet, was full of wonderful Spanish melodies and a clutch of musical jokes – some of which were far too clever for me. Sue and I devised a dramatic act to go with the words and music and, before we knew it, we were performing it to primary school children in Devon. Sue was the narrator, Bill played Eric the Rabbit and I was the evil matador, with remaining parts filled by other friends. Andy Feist was the horn player in the touring wind quintet and, as part of the educational experience, he wowed the school children with a loud and high rendition of the theme from *Star Wars*.

The Tale of Eric the Rabbit on tour in Devon (See page 149)

Graham used his music for Eric as part of his composition portfolio for his degree. Because of this, and not just for my vanity, we decided to record the whole of Eric's words and music on tape. We assembled on the stage in the university great hall, where the acoustics were quite good, although Graham's tape recorder was not quite so good. The microphone was unable to cope with Andy's very loud and very high solo on the triumphant version of 'Eric's theme' and the recording goes a bit fuzzy at this point. Furthermore Helen, the usual bassoonist in the Eric Quintet, was unavoidably detained that lunchtime and so Sue had to whip out her bassoon and sight-read the part. This left me to narrate the words. I knew them well enough, but was less sure of some of the cues from Graham of when to come in and when to shut up.

Eric the Rabbit turned up again a few years later in a fund-raising concert in Hampstead's Burgh House. Graham's original music was cleverly rearranged by composer Adam Gorb for the trio of instruments we had to hand, which were piano, flute and violin. The old original cassette recording was even digitally remastered last year but, sadly, Andy's levels of high and loud were beyond salvaging and you still can't hear anything else, including the words.

My dissertation for my English degree was inspired by Eric. I did some limited research on 'The History of the Rhymed Couplet'. I had enjoyed studying Chaucer, Pope and Crabbe. Therefore I was quite interested to discover in what a deliberate and calculating way Keats and Shelley had set about dismantling the rhymed couplet as the symbol of classical poetry to replace it with the new Romantic Movement. I just thought they were wishy-washy airheads who loved clouds and flowers. Apart from the odd diehard like John Betjeman, who admitted that using rhymed couplets helped him to think of new ideas because of the need to find a rhyme, the form was out of fashion. My dissertation concluded that: "The rhyme, in its traditional couplet, has reached the end of the line".

Like Graham, I also submitted *Eric the Rabbit* as part of my creative portfolio at the end of my English degree. Eric was in there with my truly heavyweight angst poem about disability, one about a punk friend who reminded me of a stained-glass window and an ingenious poem about the beautiful colours of the rainbow that you can see in an oily puddle on a London street. When he returned my portfolio I hoped my tutor would say: "That poem about disability was very strong and very moving", but all he actually said was: "I liked the one about the rabbit".

My third year at Exeter was transformed when I met and fell in love with Emma. She had beautiful hair, a winning smile and sparkling eyes. She had played county lacrosse, liked Genesis (our tune was *Follow You, Follow Me*) and she liked to do the Telegraph crossword. A match made in heaven I thought. We met one weekend when John Hiley was down on a visit. We were looking for a tennis court and persuaded the two girls playing on the one outside Lopes girls' hall to play doubles with us. Because John is my best mate, he let me play with the pretty one, who said she was called Emma. It turned out that she was rather good at tennis and, even though I later found out all the other good things about her, I have always shared John Betjeman's attraction to the "tennis-playing, hiking girl; the greatly to my liking girl" as well as to rhymed couplets.

Saying it with ginger biscuits on Emma's birthday

The fact that she was a skilled completer of the full *Daily Telegraph* crossword should have told me that, not only was she clever and quick-witted, but also that – yet again – I'd fallen for a girl with a conservative dad. This one worked in life assurance and lived in Great Malvern, which were further clues. You will have gathered that I am not exactly communist and my stock is of Hampstead socialism rather than Hackney, but in my youth I always found the fathers of my girlfriends to be hard work. Their lack of enthusiasm for me ranged from the disapproving to the downright antagonistic. Now that my daughter Katherine is maturing I have a certain sympathy for some of these men's attitudes. I have contemplated applying for a shotgun licence to preserve my daughter's modesty in the face of the inevitable future onslaught of unwashed and unwelcome youth. No, not really, but I understand more the general principle of father-daughter relations. As it happens, this latest girlfriend's conservative father was the real deal. In the year I went out with Emma it was her father's turn to be master of the local Masonic lodge. I was invited to escort her to the Ladies' Night at the poshest hotel in Malvern. We sat through a shortened version of the mystic process that seemed a bit like Boy Scouts meet Harry Potter. I was dressed for the part, having by then acquired my own better-fitting dinner suit for the orchestra, and Emma and I quite enjoyed falling over each other in our inability to waltz, if only that we were not usually encouraged to touch each other in his presence.

Bright Eyes loves Fluffy Bun

I had a lovely year with Emma. We were soppy and in each other's pockets all the time. I wonder if our relationship was affected by the fact that Emma began to develop health problems that meant we cuddled a lot but never actually consummated the relationship which a) will probably come as a huge surprise and relief to her dad, and b) meant that there was never a sense of us using each other 'just for sex' like some relationships are... Emma was in the year below me at Exeter. I drove her down there at the start of her third year when I was about to go off to Australia on another voyage of exploration. Emma had had a successful operation that summer and we could have made love then. Perhaps sensing the slight declining arc of this particular love affair we chose just to hold each other tight before I left to go round the world.

My mother and Emma agreed to pass on my letters to each other, which they did, although we were not helped by a postal strike in Australia while I was there, meaning nothing got through for a month. Eventually I got a letter from Emma, even as I was back in Sydney preparing to fly home for her 21st birthday and clutching the opal necklace from the Australian mines. She had assumed from my lack of letters that I didn't love her anymore and she had now transferred her affections to the international windsurfer in the university flat next door. It's true that the line I had written in my letter to her from Alice Springs, saying that it was the most beautiful thing I had ever seen in the world and would only be better if she was there to see it with me, had rung a little false even as I wrote it. Prophetically perhaps, Nick Hackett was once again on the scene to be able to reassure me that there were even still plenty more fish in the sea, mate, and John Hiley asserted that it was her loss. Nevertheless I was very sad

Most of my relationships with women have taken root while John was elsewhere, mostly out of the country altogether. What does this mean? Not that he was ugly, aggressive or otherwise off-putting to women, particularly. Probably that John and I are so content in each other's company that we would be unlikely to stir to seek others, even of the fairer sex. I think it is related to the truism that the more you like someone, the more likely they are to go out with a plonker (or a wrong 'un). It is therefore a frustration when your mate spends time with his girlfriend when you could be having a proper laugh over a pint, talking about a rehash of all the old things that you always talk about. Actually my wife Mary really likes to have a proper laugh over a pint, talking about *most* of the old things that John and I talk about. Consequently she is very fond of John and vice versa, because they both like to see me happy, although she does predict the early classification of John and me as old codgers.

However John made an incautious remark that he thought Emma had a "face like a bag of chisels". I'm sure it was meant as a joke and so I incautiously passed it on. I didn't need Sandy as my "what women really mean" adviser to spot that Emma didn't think it was very funny. Later John confessed that, although he had been there at the very start of the relationship, he had never liked Emma. I wish he'd said that earlier.

Another early blow to the gloss of my relationship with Emma was when a close friend Sue explained that I couldn't be best friends with her if I'm Emma's boyfriend. She was right, of course, although I was inexperienced enough with having a girlfriend to feel rather disappointed. I was particularly pleased with a poem I wrote featuring an extended allegory about a strawberry allergy (how I love, but I can't love my favourite fruit). In turn, it transpired that Emma was jealous of the orchestra in general – and definitely not Sue in particular. Emma sent me a valentine card that year and arranged for a bogus one to be delivered from a mystery member of the orchestra, so that she could express her jealousy. She only confessed to being the author of the bogus one when two more cards also appeared to add some authenticity to the indignation. I could honestly say that I only sent one to Emma, but it just shows again how the path to true love is not smooth.

All my life, most of my friends have been women. I have had a core of close male friends, in Nick, Dave, Gareth, Derek, Bill and John, and then quite a number of other female friends. These were not girlfriends, but I have felt very close to them and I have comfortably shared an emotional literacy with them. Mostly I have felt that these people know who I am; they instinctively see through me, all the show-off sparkly bits that we all tire of quickly, and yet, rather to my surprise, they still like me. Sue was one, and Caroline Harris-Reed was another, but there have been several others too. Because they seem to know me so well, the instinct is to stay close. And yet this closeness is problematic in the exclusive relationship defined by boyfriend status. I don't really know the solution to this social quandary, without being able to take a regular lie detector test to prove that good female friends really can be just good friends.

I was on the M5 on the way to see Emma in Malvern when I heard on the radio that Caroline had been murdered. It was such a shock and I had to pull onto the hard shoulder because I needed to cry. Emma and her family were very supportive, as I really struggled to come to terms with the death of a close contemporary. Caroline was the random victim of a motiveless crime. This probably increased my sense of anger to go with the grief and loss. I had never been to the funeral of someone young before and I remember feeling sorry for Caroline's mother, who had to convert instantly from being grieving parent into gracious host to invite us back to the house. It seemed so terribly unfair, that we were forced into these polite conventions when we would prefer to be beating our breasts and tearing out our hair.

GOING DUTCH AND DOWN UNDER

MY OLD PAL JOHN Hiley used occasionally to visit me in Exeter in his old car. The electrics were particularly dodgy on the car, which meant that if the brake lights went on then the radio went off. Therefore, in order not to spoil a good song, John developed a style of driving that avoided using the footbrake at all costs. We careered around a few corners with just a little tug on the handbrake, but at least we were singing along to every word in every verse. At Exeter, we would fill the car beyond its natural capacity and sing our way out to a country pub. Because John had already graduated and was (for the first and only time in his life) in a lucrative and steady job, he bought the first round. We then clubbed together to buy the next round, and then it was John's round again – cheers John! This is when he first picked up the nickname 'Uncle John', although my children made more sense of it in later life.

In 1980, the second long vacation from Exeter, John, Bill and I decided to have a short break in Amsterdam. Continuing the theme of filling a mode of transport beyond its natural capacity to go drinking, we hatched a plan to go on a tandem. Three men on a tandem really doesn't work well, but the novelty factor was attractive. For some reason we thought to hire the tandem in London, although I'm sure we weren't planning to cycle all the way there. We found a tandem-hire shop near Victoria station and John and I undertook to ride it home. John felt confident enough to take the handlebar end, which left me as 'the engine room' although we all know that the driver can't always tell if you've stopped pedalling and are looking over your shoulder instead of his. Since you have no control over the steering, maybe it is better not to look anyway.

We were just pulling out onto the Marble Arch roundabout when the tandem first started showing signs of breaking in half. This is not a good thing. I'd never stood on the central island of one of London's busiest roundabouts before, but we had to take shelter somewhere while we reinserted the central bolt that held the tandem together. When it happened again going up Park Lane we realised that this bike wasn't going to get us anywhere – except maybe a hospital. In the end we went to Amsterdam by coach and hired a tandem (and another bicycle for the third man) from a shop with a stunning range of shiny new bikes and tandems that weren't going to convert into a unicycle at the first pothole.

Bill was keen to go to Holland to look at organs. John and I had an interest in this too. The organ Bill most wanted to look at was in the northern town of Alkmaar. This was famous as one of the best pipe organs in Europe and since Bill's main musical instrument is the organ this was quite a draw. He didn't mind coming with me and John to see the organs that we were interested in too, which were mainly displayed on the main avenue down from central station and some of the smaller premises towards the flea market, decorated outside with their pretty red lights. But perhaps one should focus on the famous old organ of Alkmaar. The three of us set out enthusiastically on our two bikes to head north. The roads were very flat. Certainly there were no problems with steep hills, or of course any hills whatsoever. After a few miles, oh! how we longed for some sort of hill. Suddenly John, who was on the back of the tandem and able to scour the horizon, spotted a cow. This was quite an event, so we all stopped to have a look. An hour or so later, Bill spotted a windmill by a lake. No wonder windmills are so highly thought of in Holland – so we celebrated this double attraction by stopping for lunch. This would probably have been one of the main highlights of the day if we hadn't lost our Frisbee in the lake.

Working in tandem – complete faith in John Hiley's driving

By the time we got to Alkmaar it was getting dark and we decided to leave one of the best pipe organs in Europe until the following day. We had nowhere to stay, so we instinctively headed for a bar to have a drink and think about having nowhere to stay. I can't remember now how we got talking to the friendly bearded man who offered us accommodation at his place, which turned out to be some sort of Christian hostel but with nobody else in it. Had I been alone I would probably have declined this offer, but with three of us we felt safe to accept. Well I must say the Alkmaar organ was very nice... but not necessarily one for which I would have chosen to spend the best part of two days in the saddle. We saw more cows on the way home.

Our first night in Amsterdam was spent in a terrible hostel. Thirty or forty people sleeping on the floor in one large room with the merest hint of a mat to keep us off the wooden floorboards. This was long before health and safety legislation became popular, but even I could see that this was a firetrap waiting to happen. For the rest of our stay we transferred to the good ship Cura. This called itself a 'floatel' as it was moored in the dock near the central station. It was a little Spartan but infinitely better than the first night. One of the curiosities of the Cura was the happy hour it offered all residents at a set time every week. Heineken was half price for the entire time it took the boat to make its weekly outing to the refuelling station up the canal. The happy hour was compensation to residents for the inconvenience of the floatel being out of position for a while. We were delighted to consume large amounts of cheap beer and it's a wonder they did not lose more Cura residents overboard most weeks.

One step better than cheap beer was free beer. This was on offer at the Heineken factory after the tour of the bottling plant. This was tolerably interesting, but the main event was still to come. While the commercial sell movie was showing at the end of the tour, the beer that the waitresses were carrying was free. This meant you had about ten minutes to neck as much as you could acquire using various tactics to waylay the waitresses. We were extremely merry as we stumbled, blinking back out into the Amsterdam sunshine. As a suitable cautionary tale against 'the demon drink' we were emboldened to travel home on the tram without buying a ticket. Everyone seemed to get on and off at every door and there were no conductors or ticket collectors to supervise payment. Needless to say, on this first occasion we didn't buy a ticket, the minute the doors of the tram closed the plain clothes inspectors swarmed over the passengers and we were nicked. Playing the ignorant foreigner cut no ice with them and when they were about to confiscate my passport it seemed appropriate to cave in and pay up. The fine cost 13 guilders, before the days of Euros of course, which made a significant dent in the holiday budget. Even with the free beer I was definitely out of pocket.

You may gather that I had done a minimal amount of research before going to Amsterdam. I knew about Van Gogh and Anne Frank, but we didn't consume either of these cultural highlights. However the cultural highlight that we did try to consume was Uitsmijter. 'A national dish in Holland' particularly popular for breakfast I had read. It was explained as an open ham sandwich topped with an egg or two, sometimes served with cheese. Perhaps it was my pronunciation, but the waiter was quickly losing patience with me when I tried to order it at a café on the Leidesplain:

> *"Uitsmijter, please mate"*
> *... (pause) ... "What?"*
> *"Uitsmijter ... a national dish in Holland...?"*
> *"What? ... oh, you mean 'Ham and Eggs' "*

There can be little doubt that the ham and eggs were delicious.

The final cultural highlight we did venture into was the red light district. Well it seemed ruder not to ... We saw *What The Swedish Butler Saw*, I fondly remembered my classical education while watching the uncut film of *Caligula* and, unlike Uitsmijter, we discovered that a brothel was not a soup kitchen or anything else to eat. This travel certainly broadened this mind a little further.

Wizard Time In Oz

After graduating from Exeter University I took some more time off to travel further afield. John Hiley had already given up the steady job for British Telecom in Crouch End and had rather curiously been employed by the Australian Standards Authority in downtown Sydney. When I still didn't know what on earth I wanted to do with my life, particularly in terms of career, flying out to see a friendly face in an exciting foreign environment was very attractive.

Cramped aeroplane seats are a challenge for any tall person, but more so for one with an artificial leg. Feet swell in flight and so do limbs without feet. Swelling is uncomfortable in shoes, but it is straightforward to slip them off and put on a flight-sock. This is less convenient when the limb is enclosed in an artificial leg and the only option is to take the leg off. Quite a few people choose to get 'legless' before or during a long flight, although usually that just means a large gin and tonic.

There is a double bind with the desirable few seats on the plane by the emergency exits that have the extra legroom. If you ask for them because you need the space for your disability, they won't let you sit there because you are automatically considered to be a liability in the case of accident. You can get on a plane earlier if you have mobility difficulties, but then they definitely won't let you have the spacious seats. I was proactively offered one recently on an EasyJet flight because I was tall and strapping, and looked like the kind of guy who could throw the plane door out into the sea if we crash-landed (which I am). But if I had let on that I was grateful because I had one leg and needed to stretch it out sometimes I would have been banished to a suitably cramped seat with all the others. Full marks then to the EasyJet air steward on the flight back from France this year. I was lucky enough to nab a seat by the exit, but I was wearing shorts and the steward spotted me. He respectfully enquired if I had an artificial limb and, when I had, he explained that rules forbade me to sit there... but only during take off and landing. He went on to find me a seat for this purpose and invited me back to the roomy seats for the rest of the flight – brilliant!

It was a desperately long flight to Australia in November 1981, especially on student rates flying Indonesian Air Garuda. The food was exotic, but the conditions were cramped and we stopped over at Frankfurt, Athens, Bangkok, and Karachi before landing in Sydney. I had a slight cold and, descending into Frankfurt, my sinuses exploded to give me a splitting headache. Just like my first school journey all those years earlier, the only comfort available was barley sugar. The threat of four more descents with four more headaches was alarming. By the time we got to Karachi I was desperate to get off the plane, but this was not allowed. I stumbled out onto the top of the aeroplane steps to breathe the very oppressive, intensely humid air bouncing off the tarmac. Rather more oppressive were the four soldiers pointing their rifles at me, so I went quietly back inside to my seat.

The person in the seat next to mine on the way to Australia was called Sheila. No great surprise there then, but it turned out that her son operated the old mechanical scoreboard at the MCG. This stands for the Melbourne Cricket Ground and is the Australian equivalent of Lords as the southern hemisphere temple of cricket. What a thrill for me and my dear mate John Hiley to be allowed to climb up inside the scoreboard during the Boxing Day test against Pakistan. We even pushed a button that changed the score! Now of course it has been replaced by an electronic version, but we were lucky enough to experience part of Australian sporting folklore. Also part of Australian sporting folklore, John and I saw Evonne Goolagong playing at Kooyong, the equivalent of the All-England Club at Wimbledon, which used to host the Australian Tennis Open. My Aussie friend Michael was duly awed when he heard of my Melbourne experiences. In his youth he too played frequently at Kooyong, although never actually got around to paying the exclusive membership fees. One day he was called over from a game of doubles by the Club Manager. "Michael, I have a concern about people playing here without paying their membership fees". But before he could confess or deny his status the manager continued: "Please could you confirm that the three other guys you are playing with are fair dinkum members?" Michael assured him they were.

My Australian tour was similar to my American tour in terms of choosing destinations based on a combination of mostly who I knew and partly where I really wanted to go. I chose Australia as my travel destination mainly because John was there, even though it meant leaving my university girlfriend Emma 12,000 miles behind. I kipped on a foam mattress in his shared house in Cammaray, North Sydney, while the jet lag wore off. It was when he deftly lobbed the baked bean can into the bin from across the kitchen that I knew for sure that I had made the right decision to come. This was relaxed and fun living! I made the usual Pommie mistake of hanging my wet wool stump-socks on the washing line in the spot to give them the most sun during the day and then watched the sun sneak off in the 'wrong' direction to leave them still damp at dusk.

Just because he was out here for a year rather than a holiday like me, John inconveniently had his job at the Standards Authority to go to. This meant that I went off travelling on my own. I was quite happy with this and anyway I had accumulated a number of obscure relatives and friends of friends to visit. I started in Brisbane staying with the mother of a friend of the mother of a girl I went to primary school with. Later I stayed with some people my parents met on a bus in Greece, the parents of one of my sister's flatmates from university and the brother of the woman that ran Student Community Action at Exeter University. This brother also had an artificial leg and a greyhound and we went to watch the latter racing. All my hosts were exceptionally generous and accommodating and held few of the hang-ups that the English have about strange people coming to stay.

In Brisbane I learned how to cook a Pavlova and tried to marvel at the city's oldest building, which was a church with a corrugated iron roof. My ageing hosts were charming and waved me off from the railway station when I headed north on the Sundowner train to northern Queensland. The story goes that a brass band used to play as the Sundowner left the station and it was so slow that you could still hear the music twenty minutes later. The Melbourne Cup was running that day (a lot faster than my train no doubt). This is Australia's Derby and they say the whole country stops for it. My train literally did and I cheerfully joined in the carriage sweepstake.

I was heading for Cairns, where some obscure relations of my grandmother were going to meet me. We had been on the train for a mere eight and a half hours, stopping at tiny stations from time to time, when the guard came through the carriages calling my name. I made myself known and he handed me a note, which read: "Harry Wade (Pom), get off at Tully". This was unexpected and unexplained, but reasonably clear in its instructions, so I decided to go ahead. Tully was a tiny station less than an hour away. Nobody else 'got off at Tully' and at first there didn't appear to be anyone else on the platform, until my cousin Ged swung into view. I didn't know I had a cousin Ged, but he identified me and said he had been asked to collect me off the train and drive me out to his parents in Atherton. He commented that we only had two good legs between us as he had recently broken one of his and was wearing a cast and using crutches. That meant I was encouraged to drive his 6-litre Holden convertible. What a beauty and a beast it was! I had never driven an automatic before but it made a good throaty roar as we drove to our overnight stop at Ged's house. When we came to our first proper hill and the engine started labouring Ged said I should change down from Drive to second gear. He didn't say: "Make sure you don't hold the shift button down on the lever", which is why I went straight through the gears and Park and into reverse. We lurched to a squealing, smoking stop and Ged decided that his leg was probably ok to drive the rest of the way home.

My cousins led a tranquil, old colonial life in Atherton. Their garden was full of bougainvillea and jacaranda trees as well as apricot and greengages that appeared in the fresh fruit salad for breakfast. I tasted my first kiwi fruit and fresh mango and we walked in the tropical rain forest nearby.

To give me a genuine Australian experience they had arranged for me to spend a few days on a friend's cattle station in the Atherton Tablelands. They were having a cattle muster, which meant rounding up their herds from the vast lands on which they were free to roam. Every day was a five o'clock start (not popular with me) with steak for breakfast, lunch and tea. This too paled quickly.

Much of the rounding up was still done on horseback by hired Jackaroos and their female equivalent called, logically, Jillaroos. However the far-flung cattle were spotted and driven towards the horses by helicopter. I'd never been in a helicopter before, let alone one with no doors. My eyesight was good and I was chief spotter. However, whenever I spotted one, the pilot swerved and veered downwards to move the cow in the right direction. This quickly proved to be the wrong direction for my stomach. I rapidly became pathologically incapable of spotting cows because it inevitably meant a violent lurch sideways and downwards that left nothing between the hole in the cockpit wall and the ground 100 feet below.

When I had thrown up in and out of the door-less helicopter and couldn't ride a horse (see above) the most useful thing I could do for them was to drive the 8-tonner horse truck back to the ranch. The instructions were: "up the hill round the back of this big rock, follow the fence off the dirt road and when the fence and the road just stop, keep going straight on and you will eventually find the ranch." Yeah, right! But I'd been a queasy, useless Pom so I wanted to do it right. The Jackaroo showed me the gearbox with the low and high settings but he left it in high, as I wouldn't need the low. I revved off up the hill round the back of the big rock and promptly slipped the gear from 1st straight into 4th and stalled it. I'd really only driven a Mini before, so a ferocious hill start in a big truck stuck in high gear proved too hard. Every time I stalled I drifted backwards a little more down the hill. I started sweating profusely at the unattractive vision of the Aussies reaction when, 20 minutes after they thought they had seen the last of me, I would reappear backwards, silently from behind the big rock, grinning apologetically like an idiot. Mercifully, I worked out how to flick the button to get it into low gear and I was able to get up the hill and off chasing the kangaroos past the giant termite hills.

Trying desperately to escape my hell in a helicopter

By the time I got back to Sydney I found my old mate Nick Hackett had nabbed my foam mattress in John's room. I was relegated to the flea-ridden sofa in the lounge, much to my disappointment, and moreso for the young Australians who actually paid rent for the rest of the house including their lounge. Nick had got to know John when they both visited me in Roehampton hospital and the three of us went out on the town in Sydney. We even stayed up late to go to a topless bar. This proved as thoroughly under-exciting as the bored barmaid was under-dressed. At 2 a.m. we capered back through Sydney, taking in a children's playground. Nick and I cheered as John, in his best white 'sharking' jeans, careered down the big slide and into the puddle at the bottom that we had seen, but he only saw with a shriek at the last moment.

A big, daft bear that just wants to be cuddled ... and a koala

By Christmas, Nick had got a job but John had got some holiday so we went travelling together in Tasmania and Victoria. In Tassie we hired a car and drove round the island on the way to spend Christmas Day with the uncle of a friend of a girl I knew at Exeter. We saw some Tasmanian Devils that looked disappointingly like placid, inflated guinea pigs. We called in at what was more or less the only pub on the south-western coast of Tasmania in the tiny port of Strahan. Here, we happened to coincide with the return of a local fishing boat after many weeks at sea. They had a bumper catch of giant crayfish, worth a packet, and because the captain had a cousin in Carlisle we were included in the 'drinks on the house' all night. Somehow we ended up as the proud owners of a giant spiny crayfish, which the captain assured us was dead. We had nowhere to stay the night so we slept in the car on the sand dunes – with the crayfish locked safely in the boot.

The next day was Christmas Eve and we drove along in the baking sun with the windows rolled down, listening to an incongruous *Jingle Bells* on the radio. No snow to dash through and the crayfish was hanging in there and not too whiffy as we drove through the Queenstown quasi-lunar landscape. Much like Parys Mountain in Anglesey, the extensive metal ore mines had wasted all vegetation leaving the land exotic hues of reds and blues. This was quite a draw for Tasmanian tourists and I gather they had to ask for a grant to spray the hillsides when the vegetation inconveniently began to re-establish itself.

We handed over the crayfish to our hosts and I must say it was quite delicious as part of the Christmas Day picnic we had on the beach. The turkey was served cold and we played England v Australia at cricket. Amid the festivities John and I had a quiet and solemn moment together to agree that hot and sunny beach cricket on Christmas Day was simply "not right", but I am extremely grateful to the Causon family for sharing their big family day with us.

My childhood Lifesaving Award finally came good when I did actually save a life, and a most valuable one too. John and I were swimming in the deserted Apollo Bay in Victoria, Australia. We had been surfing on an inflatable lilo when we found that we were being carried out to sea by a "rip" current. We agreed to strike out for the beach but John said that he didn't think he could make it pushing the inflatable. I swam over and took it off him, but soon John said that he didn't think he could make it without it either. I swam back to him and, increasingly alarmed, we both drooped ourselves sideways over the inflatable. We kicked our legs and reassured each other that we were ok. After some time, even when we didn't seem to be making much progress towards safety, we must have crossed the sand bar again and the waves returned to dash us onto the beach. We were knackered and a bit scared. But we composed ourselves enough not to tell or worry our elderly Australian hostess who had been reading the paper in the car all this time, unaware of our plight.

The final loop of my journey took me north from Adelaide to the red centre of Australia. There was no platform at the station in Alice Springs in early 1982. You just had to jump down from the train into the red dust. I had nowhere to stay but I felt so excited to be in such a rare and beautiful natural environment and I felt powerful and self sufficient because I knew I could control my life and, for starters, find somewhere to sleep that night. I found a hostel in a back street and joined in with the communal barbecue in the back garden. We all drank 'tinnies' and 'stubbies' of the favourite barbecue beer Tooth's (or it might have been Toohey's, since they tasted similarly bland). The adverts for this beer promoted its virtues with: "Low on fizz so you can slam it down fast!" Not one for the connoisseurs, clearly. I also learned the knack of trapping a mosquito on your arm by stretching the skin as it sticks its stalk into you. Unable to withdraw the funnel and with no valve to stop the flow of blood, the mozzie eventually pops. My new companions in the hostel were very taken with my special anti-mozzie leg that we agreed would leave a number of distressed insects with bent biting parts.

This popularity for the leg was a big improvement from when I first wore shorts regularly when touring in Australia. I giggled at the policemen in their shorts with their long white socks and black boots, but it was just too hot to wear trousers. The Australians did seem to give my leg a few funny looks in my shorts. When I asked one about it he said that he'd seen the very smooth pink leg I had and was a bit put out that I appeared to be shaving my legs. Once he found out that it was just plastic it was all fine. I thoughtfully drew some hairs on it with a felt pen and that seemed to help a lot. However, by this time in the holiday there was a new issue to sort out. My left leg had become quite tanned, while the right one remained pale pink (with black felt pen hairs). Nowadays I should probably travel with a bottle of "tan-in-a-tub" to spray on after a few days. Otherwise I need a succession of legs that have a gradually darker hue, like the Roald Dahl tale of the man with a series of wigs with slightly longer hair so that it appeared to grow gradually.

As the train was pulling in to Alice Springs I had seen three native Australians (Aborigines as they were called then) sat under a tree near the dried up bed of the River Todd. Alice Springs has an annual festival called Henley-on-Todd, which features boat races down the river. All the straw boaters, bunting and picnic baskets of the real Henley are reproduced for the festival that draws substantial crowds. The River Todd is almost always dried up. The boats have holes drilled for legs and the crews run to the finish line through the sand. Consequently Henley on Todd is heavily insured against rain, for the flash floods would make the water-less event a total washout.

At the hostel I set about arranging how I could travel further into the country. I was running out of time and money to go to my original target of Ayres Rock. Instead I took a day trip by bus to Simpson's Gap in the McDonnell Ranges and here I had a life-changing moment of insight and self-awareness. As I clambered over this 450 million year old rock, finding rock pools that looked like dinosaurs had drunk from them, I was profoundly struck by the humility that I was just

21 and knew nothing, nothing, nothing of the world. I still felt powerful and self sufficient in terms of looking after myself; but I also felt aware of not over-estimating my self-importance. On the flight back to Sydney I was glued to the aeroplane window, drinking in the red-earthed infinity curving over the horizon.

I think that moment of self-discovery in the McDonnell Ranges changed me. It is a psychological point of reference that I go back to at difficult times. I think it has helped me to be less selfish, although parenthood also demands this virtue. I also learned a lot about myself later from the volunteer counsellors and from the personal development training I received while working at Centre 33, the young people's counselling and advice centre in Cambridge, but this time in Australia remains very important to me.

What a wally

I WANT TWO METRE

MY HORN CAREER continued for a while after Exeter. Brass sections in orchestras are renowned for their camaraderie (as well as their heavy drinking and disdain for violins and/or flutes). I teamed up with "Deaf Ed", one of my fellow Exeter horns, to play for the Kingston Philharmonia in south London. It was Ed's left ear that was dodgy. This meant that he had a good excuse to play First Horn so that he could listen to and stay in tune with the rest of the section, traditionally seated to his right. It can also work the other way round where not being able to hear the bum notes from the bell of the horn on your left is a great relief.

The Kingston Phil was a suitably amateur orchestra for my modest talents but, rather unexpectedly, I experienced a moment of grace during a live performance of Brahms *4th Symphony*. Brahms wrote some great horn parts anyway, but somehow all four horns played a blinder that night in the parish church. At the end of the performance we looked at each other, all aglow, knowing we shared that tingly sensation of a unique experience.

I believe that everyone has magic moments. But, next to sunset over the Grand Canyon and a dhow scudding down the River Nile, this one in Kingston-upon-Thames is the most unlikely one for me.

My French horn has now been passed on to my son Matt, who has taken Grade 8 and played in an award-winning county wind band. He played it in a duet with my daughter Katherine on the saxophone while my second wife Mary and I signed the register at our wedding in 2006. Unlike me, and possibly Matt too, Katherine adds application to her musical inspiration and is charging through the grades at a relatively young age.

After Kingston-upon-Thames, my musical creativity was channelled into song-writing at the piano or, perhaps more accurately, setting my words to music. Some were clever and comic, like I Want Two Metre, about my desire for tall women:

I want Two Metre; I want to meet her,
I want to seat her inside my two-seater
And ride with my two-metre maid.

I don't court short ones; they don't last long,
I like them high, eye-to-eye with King Kong,
I brawl with small ones, we always tiff
And when they heckle my neck'll get stiff
...The higher fire me, Big Bertha's roar,
But I call small arms and legs all "small bore".

Some were clever and complaining, like *Heart Rundown*, about the fact that tall women didn't desire me:

I was standing on a corner when you walked into my street
Now I'm rolling in the gutter and I'm sprawling at your feet
I'm a single piece of litter but you say the road needs a sweep –
You cruise on in and cruise on out and cruise on by
And you always leave but you never say goodbye.

But none were clever and commercial, and we were held back by a few key factors. The positives were that John Hiley and I had got a great name for the band: The Matcho Men and, since The Pet Shop Boys only had two of them, it didn't matter that there were only two of us. In fact we were four, as we had recruited two willing "doo-wop girls" in Tracey and Fiona. Incidentally, these two have done very well for themselves, as Tracey went on to run most of Western Europe for Unilever and Fiona married an Egyptian prince. John and I have remained poor but happy. The Matcho Men's other strength was album titles and we had a fabulous collection. *Perfect Match, Match of the Day, Kids from Flame, Hasta la Vestas?*, we had them all. The potential negatives were that what we didn't have was a band, i.e. anyone who could do more than play modest piano or sing "doo-wop". Also, John didn't like my lovesick loser songs and I didn't like his songs that were all without words – apart from the one about "Hold the line", that was really a lovesick loser number. Eventually I rolled all our album cover concepts (or lame match jokes, depending on your point of view) together into one *Perfect Match*:

I used to be safety first, until I'd seen my sunburst,
I used to play my courting by the book
How dull! I was in the dark
I hadn't won not one spark...
Now turn up the gas and really start to cook!

Chorus:
It was a perfect match – no there couldn't be no catch –
Call it what you like – you can call it a lucky strike –
All the same I'm all aflame with the perfect match

I used to just swan around, boxing clever every round,
But I never was a winner when I played,
Then I met her: I'm on fire!
Boy I'm burning with desire,
Got a hotline to the local fire brigade.

John and I did actually record this together, with a Casio keyboard (drums!) and an open mike over my dining room table. Sadly, I've lost the cassette, and we were not pursued by Stiff Records, so the Matcho Men fizzled out. What a shock for Matcho Men fans that two of the three songs above were performed live at The Musician in Leicester in October 2008 in front of 75 people. For any that weren't there, you will be relieved to know that it was captured on film and is available on YouTube.

Standing tall at the 6ft dinner party

Rather more energetic was my pursuit of tall women. Music played an important part as the soundtrack to my 'Six foot dinner party'. *Long Tall Sally* by Little Richard, *Walkin' Tall* by Adam Faith and even *Walk Tall* by Val Doonican all endorsed the key message as I served the crown of lamb (with the little white hats on), whirly mounds of duchesse potatoes and a towering meringue pavlova to finish. I press-ganged in two of my taller mates that allowed me to invite three of my favourite tall women. We considered inviting John Hiley as the token short person – at only 5ft 10 – so that he could be the waiter and we could look down on him in a general way, but he declined. Despite all this effort, the tallest object of my passion still resisted my advances after I wouldn't let her drive my car simply because she wasn't insured and hadn't actually passed her test. She was delightfully long of limb but sadly short of affection for me.

This extended object of my affection was a user of my then current Camden library, St Pancras, and worked across the road. I had her details of course from her library ticket registration form, but I didn't need to loiter outside her workplace because she came into the library quite often. So besotted was I with her that I came over all trembly when she came in – clearly a lot of blood coursing round my body. The effect was that my hand was too wobbly to work the Plessey light pen that scanned the barcode on the returned books. In library terms this is known as discharging.

Getting The Hump

It is true that I mainly went into the travel agency across the road in order to engineer a conversation with a fourth six-footer who could not make the dinner party but was also a towering inferno of passion for me, although my efforts to chat her up were a damp squib. Before I knew it, Andrea had booked me on a week's package holiday to Egypt, on my own.

It was a holiday to Egypt with a difference. For a start we flew to Tel Aviv, in Israel. On the plane the air hostess plonked in front of me a tray of kosher food. When I said I hadn't ordered kosher food she checked and said that it had been specially requested by my travel operator – a special gift from Andrea, and I must say it was delicious. The nice man wearing a hat next to me on the plane was very chatty, asking about my family in Hampstead and did I have any family in Tel Aviv? I suddenly twigged that the kosher food had led him to assume that I was Jewish and when I revealed that I wasn't, he mostly talked to the man on the other side.

The next 'different' experience was the battered minibus that took us across the Sinai Desert to begin the Egyptian bit of our Egyptian holiday. I may not have read my tour leaflet properly, but the tortuous journey across the desert, past the burned out tanks and other military hardware, took many hours and I had nothing to eat or drink. Eventually we stopped at an old shack that was the local version of a service station. I was so ravenous that I bought a corned beef roll. This was a mistake. I was already feeling very dodgy as we crossed the magnificent Suez Canal. By the time we got to Cairo it was all I could do to make it up to my hotel room and I passed out. My digestive systems had taken a terrible pasting and I abandoned the sightseeing day at the Cairo museum because I was unable to move further than a couple of metres from a toilet.

Happy to be sitting down outside the Cairo Museum

Being young and relatively fit I recovered enough to join the trip out to the pyramids at Giza and onwards to the Valley of the Kings, Luxor and even up to Aswan. We had the most wonderful guide that spent some concentrated time explaining the art and the stories on the hieroglyphs while busloads of other tourists thundered in and out in the blink of a Sphinx's eye.

We travelled up to Aswan by train and, apart from having my window smashed in front of my nose by a rock thrown by some naughty kids, I discovered a beautiful sense of tranquillity and peace here. We stayed in the old hotel used for the Agatha Christie film *Death on the Nile* and the balcony had a view over the little boats on the Nile to the desert beyond. It was simply stunning.

It was less than a year since I'd returned from Australia and I was very confident about being able to travel on my own. Both the fleshy and the metal bits of the leg were in good shape and, even in my small 1980s shorts, I did not get an unseemly amount of attention from passers by. On my return to the UK I dropped into the travel agency to tell Andrea about my adventures, but I was never able to attract enough attention there either. The dysentery expert at the Royal Free Hospital was much more interested in what I had to show her.

Giza on a camel

SPORTING LIFE

TIME FOR A FINAL update on the changes in leg technology over the years. Like Jack Cosnett before him, another fitter John Talbot was inspirational at a later stage with the new generation of plastic legs. One of the greatest inventions for active artificial leg-wearers in my lifetime has been the silicon sock. You roll it on the stump and the gel keeps you safe from most of the abrasions and sores that used to afflict me from sweat-soaked cotton and wool stump socks. I was over 30 before John changed my life with this radical revolution.

The Seattle Sash and then the Dynamic Response foot have also been key developments in artificial feet since the fragile wooden blocks covered in leather that I started with as a child. They are a solid moulded piece of plastic, made out of material that is at once flexible, resilient and springy, a bit like a superball. Friends have complained that sometimes the Dynamic Response foot is more "dynamic" than I am; a bit like having another modern prosthetic development the "intelligent knee" that always wants to go to the opera when you just want to go down the pub. The new spring in my step radically improved my tennis and badminton, as well as allowing me to 'step' properly – i.e. hop on it – at a ceilidh (when Dr J_____ wasn't looking).

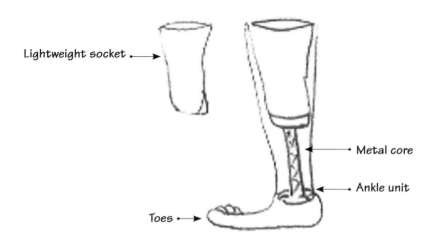

Lightweight socket →

Metal core

Ankle unit

Toes →

These were action feet. I will always be grateful to a succession of limb-fitting centre managers, a new generation on from Dr J_____, who invested their budgets in technology and equipment that I would test to breaking point in the cause of mobility. When Seattle Sash feet were relatively new and in short supply I split one playing badminton (it's still that destructive lunge to the front to play the high clear). The only replacement they had, in my size, was black rather than pink. So I became an honorary member of the Blackfoot tribe for a while.

The newer feet come with moulded toes. Rather curiously, my leg-suppliers' practice is to cover them up. I currently get a one-piece wrap of pink plastic from top to bottom of the leg. It is probably to protect the ankle, which has a join that could let in sand, gravel or water and cause damage. It was quite emotional to have toes on both sides for the very first time. I went out and bought a pair of open-toed sandals on the strength of it. I wanted to paint my toenails, only because I could. I had more or less a *pair* of feet. I'm disappointed that they instantly have to be shrouded in pink plastic.

John Talbot was always willing to try out new technology on me in an attempt to improve my quality of life. I was a good crash test dummy for any model. A completely new concept in legs came out that John wanted me to try. With this one you rolled a silicon sleeve straight on to the stump. This sleeve had a metal bolt built in to the end of it that ratcheted into a mechanism in the prosthetic leg. Once you had clicked all the way down into it, the only way out was to press the release button. This offers absolute security, no more legs falling off at inconvenient moments such as on the rugby field (although once the opposition found out about the release button they would probably be reaching for it with every tackle). However it was not a model that I took to. Although it clearly couldn't come out there was a slight stretch of the silicon sleeve every time you stepped off the leg. For a fraction of a second it felt like the leg was slipping off and I found this very unnerving. Psychologically I just could not adjust to trust it. I also had some difficulties with the slight movement around the tip of my stump. The skin on the end of my stump is still stretched tightly over the bone and walking made me uncomfortable. John was remarkably calm as we agreed to write off this new model and go back to the more familiar structure. He told me of another patient of his, a sprinter, who also rejected this sort of leg because of the millisecond of doubt in every stride.

So I've stuck to the sort of leg that isn't actually stuck to me. It means that it still could fall off at any time, although I do have a heavy-duty knee sleeve for sports made out of material like a diver's wetsuit. It slightly restricts the knee bending but at least I know it will be there for every extra active and sweaty stride. My very newest leg appears to have a shinbone, which I find pleasingly authentic, although

I seem to have knocked a few hollows into it already, which is less authentic. I'm also easily wowed by the fact that the new foot can tilt sideways, keeping full traction on a sideways slope – clever and practical!

On The Piste – Skiing

The first time I went skiing I was really fit. I was 23 and cycling to work in Euston and Holborn, which, from Hampstead, was literally downhill all the way there and uphill all the way back. It was probably the only time that the natural bulge of my calf muscle kept up with the metal bulge of my artificial leg and my knees were in great shape.

My skiing companions were my old mate John, Peter – PLJ as he is always known, Mark and Jane. John, Peter and Mark were all at University College School together in Hampstead. I might have been there too, my parents offered it to me, if one of my friends at New End hadn't sneered that UCS stood for United Cow Sheds, so I went to William Ellis instead to stick with my mates. We went Tyrolean bowling as part of the ski holiday package. A loud man called Barry appointed himself team captain and, in an effort to look cool and to impress the pretty holiday rep, he called himself Baz on the scoreboard. We were on his team so he told us to call out our names. At that moment I first became Haz (along with Joz, Pez, Maz and Jaz). Like many things that carry irony when first introduced, Haz has stayed with me since. It was my computer game name when I got into the top ten scores at Asteroids and the software only had capacity for three letters. As the capacity increased it expanded to Hazapper and then Hazapperoony, which I still use with my children when we go tenpin bowling. My joint email with my wife Mary is amusingly labelled haznmaz and, bang up to date, my Wii mii character is called Hazii. You may appreciate the second level of ironic use of the ii ending on top of the hilarious Haz root, which was only introduced in the first place to take the mickey out of Barry the Tyrolean bowler.

After much après-ski schnapps, Mark related the story of how, as a boy, he once dressed as a scarecrow. He slipped on an old jacket with a broomstick across his back and down the sleeves and ran down the garden to play. About half an hour later Mark's mother was missing him and went to see how he was getting on. She found him face-down in the flowerbed, where he had tripped when he first came out. For the rest of the time he had been laying there, arms outstretched, completely unable to recover. I have also seen a real scarecrow with someone's old artificial legs dangling off the bottom – another tilt at realism to keep the birds off the crops.

The next time I went skiing, the twisting and buffeting of the snow tweaking my right ski meant my right knee gave way when I was up the mountain. The main positive from this was that I was carried down draped over sweet-smelling and jolly attractive ski instructor Monique. All my mates started going down like ninepins, gasping and pointing at their knees in the hope of enjoying a similar favour.

A gently-sloping field in Kitzbühel

But the most disastrous skiing incident I had was when I fell and twisted my knee on my fourth and last trip. Even the new shorter skis are unstable when attached to a leg without an ankle; the tension in the knee cannot hold a ski straight if the edge catches wrongly and the ski turns suddenly. I felt my knee twist as I fell, the ski acting as a wrench. I picked myself up gingerly and started to make my way down using my trusty 'snowplough' position, even though it was an extreme painful effort to get my knee round far enough into the middle. The following morning when I clipped my boot back into the ski it became clear why so much painful twist had been needed. The impact of the fall had twisted the plastic foot outwards by 45 degrees and it was now stuck in this position. In desperation I took the leg to the ski-hire centre in the small resort. The man there spoke no English, and I tried to explain in fractured French my problem:

"Excusez-moi monsieur, mon pied est tourné a droit par 15 degrees."
"Tu veux de l'anasthetique?"
"Non merci, mais avez vous un couteau et un Allen Key?"

Once the two-man wrenching had failed to shift the foot, the only alternative was to go in with the sharp knife to locate the retaining screw that I'd watched the skilled fitters use over the years to get the foot alignment right. The screw was now buried in sculpted foam and covered with a cosmetic pink rubber skin. The Frenchman covered his eyes as I plunged the Stanley knife into my leg and after a few goes found the screw. The foot was returned to the front and he ceremoniously presented me with the Allen key in case it went again and I needed it up on the slopes. I left the shop patched up with packing tape and looking "well hard". Another tale for someone to tell their grandchildren and I took him a crate of Heineken for fixing the parts other ski-hires never reach.

I did ski again that holiday, although I have relegated skiing lower in my choice of active holidays. I haven't tried bungee jumping yet, mainly because I fear the rope will return to the top with my leg still attached and I'll be in the river. I also went skiing again a few years ago in France in the most bizarre circumstances: in a leisure park in a converted old quarry, on a dry ski slope with the weather at 40°C. We were fully clothed with an additional blue boiler suit over the top to prevent friction burns. We were pulled up by a real ski-lift and slipped down the little nursery slope, and my sons even negotiated the big slope that went most of the way back up the quarry walls. There was a moment of alarm when big son appeared at the bottom of slope without smaller son, but in tearful reunion – at least for me – he finally made it (like Buster in the film *The Incredible Journey*) having dropped a pole and he wondered what the fuss was about. You can get hot skiing in the snow when it's freezing, but wearing two sets of clothes in summer in the south of France made me melt.

I quit the French quarry ski slopes early because the leg was so slippery that the ski was getting to the point of being able to choose freely its own direction, without even the knee being able to control the swivel; shades of the film The Exorcist when the leg can turn 360°. It is very dangerous if your leg falls off and distracts the other skiers. It is also dangerous to distract dentists, and I now warn my dentist that my leg may fall off because of the angle it protrudes off the reclining chair. Heather Mills McCartney claimed that her leg fell off in public in 2005 because she got hot, and not because of a scuffle with Jennifer Lopez's security guards. I'm with Heather on this one.

I'm also with Heather on her insistence that artificial limbs should not just work well but look well too. An article about her in a Sunday magazine first alerted me to the visually pleasing shape of her 'evening wear' leg, which was slim, shapely and the foot set at an angle for a relatively high stiletto. The cosmetic appearance of prosthetic legs has improved considerably in the last twenty years, not just with smooth plastic coating replacing flaking pink metallic paint.

There is a movement in the ranks of the artificial limb-wearers with the tag line "Naked not faked". It is a bold and confident stance that says: "Yes, of course I've got a disability, so what?" I suppose I am in that mode when I wear my shorts, but I do like to have a choice. There was an earlier campaign for people with disabilities that promoted the line "Take a picture, it lasts longer". In other words, "Don't just stare furtively, go the whole hog with a photo". The trouble these days, with the amount of mobile phones with cameras and the slackening of respectful good manners, you would be digitally recorded on the spot. I appreciate that, for ex-model Heather Mills and for other women, there is a further tyranny in society of being judged on having 'good legs'. If only this meant 'mechanically sound and didn't squeak' we'd be alright, but clearly some women with artificial legs will feel constrained from wearing skirts and dresses, and Scotsmen with kilts, and tennis players with shorts.

Another dimension to this came in a recent trip to Botswana. Nearly everyone wears shorts because it is so hot. A South African man, who was staying near us had a 'naked' leg, with no cosmetic pink padding. However his socket carried a striking modern art design in the chequered style of Mondrian. It was saying not just "don't look at my leg", not just "it's ok to look at my leg" but "look at my leg!" Without thinking I said out loud: "Wow, look at that leg!" Now, as it happens, I *was* wearing trousers that first evening and he would not have known instantly that I too had an artificial leg. But he still responded positively along the lines of how proud and appreciative he was about the skill of the design and the technology that he wanted to show it off. He made the fitting of it sound like a close relationship with a tailor in the making of a Saville Row suit. I was very impressed.

Short Leg – Cricket

Short leg or long leg? This is the obvious choice for my fielding position in cricket. I'm an inexperienced cricketer; I used to play just once a year in the annual

Wade's Wanderers game against the village of Dean and now I play even less. My inexperience showed when, rather than bending down and fielding the ball with my hands as it sped towards me, I stuck out a leg. The ball hit me on mid shin area and all the players winced on my behalf in anticipation of the pain. But of course with such plastic padding and metal core in my defence the ball rebounded rapidly towards the batsman and we were a little unlucky not to get a run out.

This sort of protection also allows me to bat without wearing cricket pads. Pads are heavy, cumbersome things and as a left hander, leading with my right leg I really don't need them. The lack of pads balances out the fact that I am not allowed a runner to help me when batting. This is because I entered the field of play with my 'impairment' rather than acquiring it when already out there. I do wonder if I should get round this rule by hopping out to the middle and putting my leg on at the crease. I'm not particularly well built for 22 yard dashes with a sprint start. Again, exercise in the summer weather means that slippery stump socks could lose me the leg when running between wickets. The only upside of that is that I could dive with the leg in outstretched arms in front of me to make my ground.

I have honed the ability to hit the cricket ball by playing 'apple slogging' under the big apple tree in Dean. This entertaining game involves lobbing up the rotten windfall apples for the batsman to slog. The harder apples will go for miles but the rotten ones will disintegrate on impact and shower the batsman. For a batsman to 'pick' the really soggy apples is the same skill as spotting the googly – it's the one to leave rather than follow with the bat. Everyone ends up smelling deliciously of cider.

1 Wood – Golf

I don't really play golf much – but I do have a handicap. A golf club banned a disabled member from driving round the course in his buggy during a tournament because getting tired by walking a long way was part of the challenge. I've already said that I'm not keen on long walks, but my main difficulty is holding the skinny golf club with a couple of right hand fingers that don't bend well.

I am happy enough with my inconsistency to go on a golf range and belt the ball as hard as I can. Sometimes the ball will go a long way and sometimes I ground the club, the ball squirts sideways and the impact judders up my arm. In Biarritz I visited a golf range that was imaginatively set on a lake. One hit golf balls at various floating islands and targets and then, at closing time, a man chugged round in a boat with a drift net and hauled the catch in. The only left-handed

7-iron they had for hire had a wooden shaft. On my 34th swipe, the club grounded badly, there was a loud crack and the head of my 7-iron twirled forwards into the lake. It sank without trace. I prepared to face the wrath of the hire shop: "Desolé, la tete de mon sept-feu est au fond du lac...". I'm not sure if the French was very accurate, but they seemed to understand my situation and better still they saw the funny side of it.

Court In The Act – Tennis (And Badminton)

My leg fell off in the middle of a tennis rally once in Sheffield. It was sweaty and slippery, as above, and I took off to my left to retrieve a wide ball and found "I hadn't got a leg to stand on". But at least I won the point because the opponent was watching me rather than the ball when he tried to play the volley.

This is the desperate end of how to win at tennis. Another good trick for getting back into matches is to take the leg off when changing ends and tip the sweat out onto the court, as this can really unsettle opponents. The opposition should drop-shot me less, as I've got a long reach and usually get them, but should lob me more because although I'm tall I'm not as springy as I might be and I'm slow to turn. They should also try to play me on a hot and sweaty day, if their concentration is good.

The psychology of tennis is interesting. People (and especially Australians) do get frustrated and hate to be beaten by a person with one leg. Those who know me will tell me about it; those who don't know me tend to say: "you do ever so well!" I try hard not to find the "ever so well" lines patronising, and some clearly mean it positively. I believe there should be enough to admire in my game (on a good day) and I sometimes want to point out that drawing attention to my disability can be considered offensive.

However when I joined a new badminton club recently I decided to play the first few weeks in tracksuit trousers. Despite risking the "slippery when wet" syndrome, I wanted the other members to find out about my game first before they found out about my disability. I always wear shorts, for comfort, at my tennis club and I think I am generally less self-conscious about my legs than my teenage son is about his. I just prefer to concentrate on the merits of the tennis (or badminton) rather than how many legs the players have.

Part of the conversational gambit in tennis is to complain about injuries. The nearest I get to passing back the "you do ever so well" comment is to respond to "I've hurt my ankle" with "I've got a spare one in the car".

I suffered a nasty knee injury playing tennis a few years ago. I slipped and fell, the plastic foot twisting my knee like a torque wrench. It went up like a balloon and I couldn't wear the leg for a week or so afterwards, nor drive, nor carry much, etc. It came as a shock to us all, I think, how comprehensive this disability of having one leg was. Dr J____, for it was he, told me that I needed to take more care and that my tennis days were over. I was devastated. However, Jack Cosnett, the fitter who was so instrumental in getting me mobile in the first place, offered me an alternative scenario. "The doctor is always right... but you never know, you might one day find yourself next to a tennis court, and you might find that you have a racket in your hand, and you might think: well, I might as well go onto the court and have a hit". And that's exactly how it happened....

My abilities to win at tennis and badminton are far more limited by my head than by my hand or leg. I read *Tennis: The Inner Game* to try to stop me being put off by opponents petty cheating or by me getting angry with myself. I do believe that the body can do most things if the mind will only let it. Having said that, the book nearly did my head in and I had to take a break from competitive tennis for a couple of years. I don't want to 'win ugly' I want to win playing the beautiful game, as far as my head and body will allow. There are some interesting parallels here with the attitude to disability. Belief and determination can go a along way to change defeat into success.

The extent of my trophy cabinet is a modest green plastic (imitation marble) thing with a genuine glued-on metal badge and three mini wooden shields. The green plastic trophy I won as a 16 year-old when I triumphed in the Globe Tennis Club under-16s event. Another former winner of this title is Davis Cup player Alex Bogdanovic. In the final I played a 12 year-old who had already been heavily beaten in the semi finals. However rain intervened and his conqueror had to go back to public school when the final was postponed. My victim was reinstated only to be swept aside 6-1 by me. So uneven was the contest that the sprinkling of club members watching clapped more loudly for the loser's one game won than for my inevitable final victory.

Ten years later I won my other two tennis trophies in the same year; in fact on the same day. My local club was called the Muswell Hill United Reform Church Lawn Tennis Club. There were not many members, not least because, with a name like that, writing your cheque to pay your membership required considerable commitment; but one could hope for a whopping trophy for the annual tournament if only to fit the club name on it. For London, there was a superficially homely and parochial feel to the club. The vicar would come to present the prizes for the annual tournament and I took part in the 'cake rota' for Saturday afternoon's mix-in. Underneath, there was a strict club hierarchy as the

Normal service will be resumed ...

club was mostly run and dominated by the twin dynasties of the Smiths and the Browns (as we shall call them). To be fair they put a huge amount of work into maintaining four good quality red shale courts, but they expected their dues in return. I was made first team captain and we won promotion to the giddy heights of North Middlesex League Division Six. But my name was mud, because I picked a team without a single Smith or Brown in it. On finals day the clans were restive as my pal Robin and I blew away a couple of Browns (or was it Smiths?) in the men's doubles and then, after my nervy start, Robin beat me in the men's singles. The trophies had been made particularly small that year. I received two identical mini wooden shields. One had a stick-on plastic panel that said MHURCLTC Men's Doubles Winner and the other one that said MHURCLTC Men's Singles R-Up. In the years to come these won't be troubling the Antiques Roadshow.

Although as incomers we alienated the stalwarts of the club, Robin and I had a wonderful time playing tennis with two other non-Browns/Smiths called Janet and Mary. We travelled to faraway places like Ealing and Gordon Hill (didn't he used to play for Man Utd?) in the London Knockout Cup. Janet played like a bloke and she and Robin were all bristling aggression. For us, Mary mopped up at the back while I pranced around at the net, perfecting my 'lunge and leave' technique. Mary had three charming daughters who were around my age and played a bit of tennis, but it was their mother who would have dominated the 'fantasy mother-in-law' conversations in the MHURCLTC locker room – had it not been half a garden shed and only divided from the ladies half by a flimsy piece of hardboard.

My last trophy is for badminton. I won the London NALGO Open Badminton Mixed Doubles Cup Plate. Having played out my nerves by being knocked out of the cup competition proper, and partnered by the helpfully ruthless Jan, we stormed through the 'plate' competition to win triumphantly.

In 1989 I was invited to join the badminton squad training for the forthcoming paralympics. I declined, partly because of the imminent birth of my first child and partly because I wasn't sure if I preferred to be mediocre in able-bodied badminton rather than excellent in a disabled group. The wise old boy, Dennis, who ran the badminton club in Muswell Hill, counselled me that I could surely be both. But I decided to spend more time with my new family instead. Here ended my collection of tennis (and badminton) trophies.

Driving Range – Not Golf

I do actually have a trophy for driving go-karts, but it was hardly won on merit. A group of friends went karting for the first and only time and, because one of us knew the owner, he arranged for our leading team to get a prize. Out of six teams on the night, my team was fifth... but our other team was sixth – Result! Apart from that, driving has been more for work than for sport, although I did once have a car that looked sporty...

Like aeroplane and theatre seats, I also didn't really fit into the driving seat of my Ford Puma, although this was the car I have most loved. The tight fit was mainly because of my height rather than the artificial leg and I considered the discomfort was worth putting up with for the Puma's sporty purr. The leg has restricted me from driving some types of car altogether. I tried to test-drive a Mazda but it had such a wide armrest on the door that my leg kept getting jammed between it and the steering wheel. I also didn't get far in an Alfa Romeo where the pedals were too close together for my artificial leg to be certain of hitting the right one. I very recently found out about the Disabled Driving Association's guide to cars that gives all the key dimensions, which is a fabulous, if under-publicised resource.

I only joined Camden Libraries & Arts Service in 1978 to earn money to holiday in the USA. Ten years later I worked my last year for them driving the Camden Link, a 40-ft long articulated lorry. It was made out of feather-light aluminium, not far off tin foil, to keep it from tipping the scales and being classed as an HGV. The concept was a clever, modern approach to libraries. It was a logical extension to the old library van that took books to housebound readers. This flexible trailer initially took a wide range of library materials to the new and isolated Maiden Lane Estate, and it still had room at the back for a private space for a Citizens Advice advisor. Like Thunderbird 2's collection of pods, the idea was that the van could drop the library at Maiden Lane, take another trailer to run a promotional visit to a Kilburn school and then park a hologram exhibition in Tottenham Court Road.

Because it was so light, the driver did not legally require an HGV licence and so could be staffed entirely by library workers and not require a Works Department driver. My colleague Neal and I came out of the Community Information Services team to be the first Mobile Librarians. Our basic training consisted of a week driving over cones (was supposed to be round them) in the old Wembley Stadium car park... and then we were allowed to take it home. I really enjoyed the new challenge of learning to handle such a big vehicle in such small spaces available in Camden. It was a particularly good brain teaser game reversing an articulated lorry round a corner and straightening up by turning the wheel towards the back end you can see sticking out in your mirror. Of course it was also a gambling game played where the 'chips' were on the other cars' paintwork.

There was never a problem about having an artificial leg here; the problem was far more about getting stuck sideways across busy roads. The first week we went to Maiden Lane at lunchtime I brilliantly (if I may say so) squeezed the Camden Link forwards into the tight access road lined with cars and into the space that we had coned off during the morning. We had leafleted the estate and we had a reasonable dozen or so new library users to show for our outreach ("Outreach – I'll be there" was our song). So far so good. Every subsequent time we came to Maiden Lane we made sure we reversed into the access road, as on this first time it proved impossible to back out. Wedged between the parked cars we couldn't get the angle on the cab to back round the corner again out into Agar Grove. Agar Grove in the rush hour is a main thoroughfare out of Camden. I was stuck across it for about twenty minutes, and I learned a few new swearwords from local commuters, until three men helped Neal to bounce a couple of cars right onto the pavement to give me the width I needed to turn. We always planned our 'exit strategy' more carefully after that.

I still got stuck perpendicularly across a bus route off Kilburn High Road a few months later, although this time a bus driver, who did have an HGV licence, sorted it out for us. That was a bad day, not because of getting stuck, which happened quite a lot, but because on the way home I just clipped the tail-light of a car parked in a narrow West Hampstead road. Again, just clipping things happened quite often, which is why we always travelled with a tub of T-Cut, the paint restorer. Sadly, this particular tail-light belonged to the leader of London's governing body the Greater London Council, who caused a terrible fuss. "What was an unqualified librarian doing driving a 40-foot long articulated lorry down a small residential road in West Hampstead?" he demanded. Fair question, some would say... I wanted to point out that actually, by then, I was a fully qualified librarian, having chartered with an M.A. from Sheffield University. But Camden just apologised profusely in order to keep the service from being permanently parked up.

Having a clean and unrestricted driving licence to show and an unmodified car has meant a largely happy and trouble-free time for me behind the wheel, with no questions asked. I could take and pass the cursory Minibus test for local authorities ("Can you back this round the corner? Well done, you passed!") that allowed me to ferry old folks to the Hampstead Community Centre Christmas Dinner. A clean licence is often stated as essential for some jobs and I spent a huge amount of time in my car as Regional Development Officer for Suffolk with the National Association of Citizens Advice Bureaux (now called just Citizens Advice). I was constantly haring between barmy Beccles and sultry Sudbury (ah, those memories of that hot damp smell of the dog-biscuit factory!). In total I calculate that I have driven over half a million miles in my life. Quite a carbon footprint from a carbon fibre leg.

It is particularly helpful to have a standard, uncomplicated driving licence for car hire in foreign airports. I always wear trousers and there's no need to explain anything in fractured Portuguese. The only misunderstanding I had recently was at a car hire in Menorca. In the usual flurry as a plane-load of punters hit the desk at the same, the flustered assistant was searching for Harry Wade in the box file on the other side of the office. "Harald Wankë?" she bellowed, to much guffawing in the shop. I pointed out my real name, the fact that the one suggested was quite rude in Britain, and that Harald was probably a German on the next Lufthansa flight. I am pleased to say that we got a free upgrade to a car with air conditioning.

TWO LEGS GOOD, ONE LEG BETTER?

FOR A VERY LONG time I had a strong feeling that having an artificial leg would somehow automatically protect me from further serious health problems. It sounds like a football superstition that my son Rob and I had: that Chelsea would never lose if we picked up two pots of 'lucky' UHT milk from a Burger King on the way to watch the game. So while my sister jumped off a chair and broke her arm, and fell off a fairly large beachball and broke her collarbone, the most I have done is sub-lux (slightly dislocate) my shoulder chasing a plastic duck on an icy day. We were conducting trials for the first ever Dean Duck Dash, which I had organised as a fund-raiser for the Eileen Wade School (named after my granny). In wintry conditions, the plastic pilot duck had covered the distance down the swollen brook in lightening speed and if it had skidded across the icy ford it would have been off and running for Kimbolton five miles away. I darted towards the ford to head off the duck but slipped on the ice in a classic slapstick fall. The bad news is that I had to go to casualty for the only time in my life, but the good news is that we caught the duck before it got away.

So, one leg better, in this case? Possibly... although Chelsea lost to Barnsley last year despite us having the requisite lucky milks and, at 50 years old, I'm not over-confident that my health is fully protected just by having an artificial leg. My positive frame of mind is probably much more potent.

Having an artificial leg can definitely attract attention. Throughout this book I have looked at being looked at, because of my leg or my hand. I have rarely sought to draw attention to it, usually quite the reverse, but it does draw other people's care or curiosity. Children, and especially siblings, often compete for attention. And older siblings regularly feel pushed out of the limelight by the arrival of a younger brother or sister. A family friend, Ben, aged 9, asked at school to do a painting of his family, sketched daddy, mummy, older sister, older brother... and the two cats. In cunning Stalinist mode he thus eradicated belated younger brother, Olly, aged 4. Those five golden years of being the youngest and fairest were too good to abandon when they could be recreated with just a little artistic licence.

As well as all the broken bones, my sister Joanna has sometimes brought up the comparability of her disadvantaged childhood – of being the sibling of a child with special needs, as she puts it. There are three scenarios: I can see that people may have made a special fuss of me if they thought I needed extra encouragement; it may be the cursed lot of the elder child, where the youngest child always gets the attention; or that our parents told us both equally that they loved us and that only I believed them every time. For whatever reason, Joanna felt sometimes less in the sunshine when she was growing up and I felt bathed in warm love and affection. If this was the grain of sand in her oyster, coupled with her talent and industry of course, she has worked her socks off and gone on to achieve brilliant things. She starred in the title role of Ibsen's *Peer Gynt*, a one-man show more or less and a peculiar choice for an all-girls school were it not for Joanna's prodigious acting prowess. Apart from going with my parents to watch the show, I was also her special adviser in how to deliver the line: "Look at that sparkling flock of girls!" as she wanted to make it more leering and lewd – my speciality. Her specialities turned out to be in the fields of homelessness, where she was a driving force in creating the major charity Crisis (formerly At Christmas) and discrimination law where her work has challenged and changed legislation for the better. For this she has received the MBE from the Queen and I'm very proud of her.

I was very proud of Joanna too when I turned up at her 40th birthday party to see the rural pub garden packed with so many of her friends. There were groups from various parts of her life and some didn't know each other well so I drifted between tables in a proprietorial "I-am-Joanna's-brother" kind of way. When I introduced myself to a group of women at one table there was a short silence. Then one of them said: "Oh, so it's you!" It turned out that they had heard a lot about me, as that sibling with special needs, in Joanna's therapy group. We chatted for a while, although I don't remember now what we talked about, but it was good to square the circle. Maybe it's as Oscar Wilde said: "There's only one thing worse than being talked about, and that's not being talked about.

So, one leg better, in this case? Maybe, although of course from time to time I've wished I had two legs, and wondered if I might have been a better sportsman. I reflected earlier that the quality time I had with my mother on our regular trips to Roehampton were 'bought' by having a disability.

Having an artificial leg can make you famous. This is not another reference to Heather Mills McCartney, as her artificial leg was one of the few things that the press did not have a go at her for in the furore of her split with Sir Paul. However, I have met graduates of Exeter University who I never knew when I was there but who said that "of course they knew of me because of my leg". A disconcerting number of people at the tennis club seem to know my name even though I don't recognise them at all.

So, one leg good, in this case? Well, I get a bit spooked by it, feeding my paranoia that I can't remember names and faces. I'm famous, or infamous, but, like Joanna with her MBE, I want to make sure it is for the right reasons. Virtue, achievement, skill, honour – yes! Artificial leg – not really!

SITTING ON MY RIGHT HAND

I SOMETIMES WONDER if I might have been right handed. Because the right hand doesn't work as well as the left hand, I've always used the left hand for everything. There's a poignant song by Dory Previn called *Left Hand Lost*, in which she describes being born left-handed but made to use her right hand at school (as indeed was my mother). She asks what her left hand might have achieved if it had been allowed to develop. My left hand is strong and my hand-eye co-ordination is really quite good, but my handwriting is terrible and has always been painfully slow. This cost me dearly in exams when I simply couldn't get down on paper in the time allowed all the things I wanted to say. Would it have made a difference if I could have held a pen with my right hand? The two fingers simply don't bend enough to hold, let alone control a pen. We'll never know, and in some ways it represents a handy half-excuse for my woeful exam marks. It's convenient to forget that my mother and sister were both born left-handed. Nothing to do then with me not revising enough and dreaming of my girlfriend in the exam hall when I should have been writing furiously...

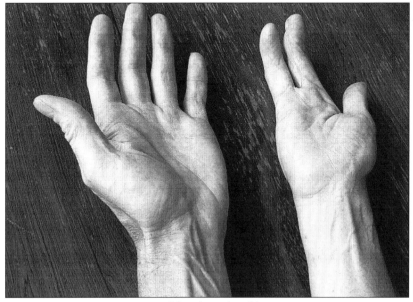

Both hands on the table

Unlike my leg, which remains largely hidden and unknown in my trousers, the hand is a very public manifestation of disability. My mother designed and knitted me a 3-fingered glove so that I wouldn't have two empty fingers flapping on my right hand. This was a very nice touch that fooled the eye of the casual observer and prevented the trailing fingers getting caught in machinery or snagged on blackberry bushes.

There is a part of me that is relieved that people do not shake hands as often as they used to. Do they think I'm a Mason when they feel the slim half-hand enclosed in theirs? If I can, I go for the manly squeeze around as much of their hand as I can span, but I often see their eyes flicking down to check why that handshake didn't feel quite right. For the super-psycho interpretation, it can feel discomforting for someone to get and give a non-regulation handshake, which is the opposite of the reassurance that it is supposed to give (and not just the apparent origins of proving that I haven't got my sword in my hand). Maybe it's just me that feels uncomfortable and disadvantaged. So I have got quite good at the German/Japanese bob/bow, and I'm always in favour of the Gallic kiss (can't really say French kiss here), but I live in fear of the high-five (three), big-up fist-touching routines. I sometimes subconsciously hide my hand in my trouser pocket, tuck it under my thigh or under the table. I also seem to keep it pinned to my side, which is counter-productive because it actually draws more attention to it.

I am however positively moved by explicit inclusion of my hand. In an art therapy module of some training I went on with Centre 33 I drew a picture of my hand being held by Jane, my first wife, in our early years. I entitled it *Acceptance* as it felt like I didn't need to hide it anymore. As I got to know Mary, my second wife, I offered her my left hand to hold over the restaurant table; but as she clasped this she asked for my right hand too, to hold "all of me". I was very moved. Physical touch and acceptance remain very important for me to feel good about myself.

I'm very taken with the Transactional Analysis theory of each one of us needing a certain number of 'strokes' each day. I understand that this does not literally mean physical strokes, although in my case these count double. It is about how we judge our worth on how others respond to us. A 'positive stroke' is when someone says or does something good to us. This is worth one point towards our individual tally that we require for the day to feel good about ourselves, which varies widely between different people and at different times.

If you can't get a positive stroke then a negative one will have to do – at least you are noticed and acknowledged. Attention-seeking behaviour is often all about this. Every day we set out anew to collect our desired tally of strokes. I would suggest that my personal required tally of strokes is quite high. I am confident that I give positive strokes very well and I am grateful to Joan, a volunteer counsellor at Centre 33, for teaching me how to accept compliments without diluting the stroke by denial. I have also been told that I am a great cuddler, which I inherited from my parents and, under the right circumstances, I can stroke with either hand.

So what are the positives of a small hand? Well of course it means it fits through smaller openings than a normal hand: down the back of sofas, blocked pipes and I never have to undo my button on my right hand shirt cuff. However cufflinks and small buttons on the other sleeve are a complete swine with stiff little fingers.

I picked up a tennis injury to my left hand – not holding the racket firmly enough on a sharp volley – and sprained tendons on my wrist. It hurt to pick up a kettle and I began to fret about how much I could use my right hand in the event of the left one being out of action. I asked the doctor if it was possible to improve the functionality of my right hand to cover for my left – and I also had an ambition that a better grip on the ball might improve my service toss at tennis. The National Health Service, having generously spent thousands of pounds on my leg over the years, suddenly opened its consultancy and treatment doors for my hand. I was referred to a 'hand specialist', who agreed that the fingers didn't bend much, sent me for an x-ray and referred me on to the cosmetic surgeons at another hospital.

I was originally hopeful that the x-rays might show a lump of gristle or bone blocking the natural movement of the finger joints. My fantasy had it that this lump could be removed with keyhole surgery and that the dormant tendons could be coaxed into life by physiotherapy. But the registrar at the next hospital had considerable doubts that any surgery was worthwhile.

It may be helpful to explain how my right hand works, and sometimes doesn't. My right thumb works very well. The joint started to get sore a couple of years ago, in a wear and tear sort of way, but taking Glucosamine has cured this. The thumb counts as 60% of the hand in official assessments. The two fingers are shorter and chunkier than their equivalents on the left hand and both fingers hyper-extend backwards up to 90 degrees, which is rare. My first finger is longer than the outside one. The first finger bends forwards from the knuckle, as it should. The middle joint will bend inwards a bit if pushed by something else and the top joint will bend outwards a bit if pushed but not inwards at all. I can tighten the tendon along the whole finger, which gives it a little strength up to the tip, but I can't move the finger on its own, although that is mainly because of the extra amount of skin in the 'saddle' between the two fingers. I'd give the first finger about 2% out of the 10% usually given to each of the four fingers.

The second finger I can waggle from the middle joint and this movement allows it to pick up the first finger on the way to make the basics of a clench. The thumb follows up on top to pull both fingers into a fist that, in the palm, has some significant strength. There is no way that I can hold onto anything by my fingertips. I'd give the outside finger about 8%, making a total of 70% for the hand as a whole.

To his credit, the registrar gave my hand a thorough examination, asked a range of questions and I felt thoroughly impressed with the service I had been given, as his last patient running late into a Friday afternoon. Before making a definitive decision on the merits of hand surgery, he referred me to the occupational therapy department for assessment.

The occupational therapist again gave me an impressive amount of dedicated time. The department is more used to dealing with patients soon after a trauma and operation to help them to compensate for loss of function, whereas I had never known full function and had learned to adapt over 45 years. Initially the therapist focussed on the scar tissue where the two fingers had been separated from their webbed state when I was a baby. The fingers are further shortened by the saddle of skin that is a remnant of the web. We all have a little bit of this at the base of our fingers where they join. She made me a mould that gently pushed back the skin at the saddle and also held in place some magical gel that helped to moisten and clear scar tissue. This was held in place by purpose-built strapping to wear overnight and keep the hand rigid. I noticed some slight improvement but, without wishing to sound ungrateful, this was not addressing the bend in my fingers, or lack of it.

A more significant session for me was when I was put through a manual dexterity test to assess exactly what one can do with one's hands. It is a sign of my competitive nature that I respond so eagerly to a set task and a stopwatch. Here was large slab of wood with nailed-on purses to open and fumble in, keys to turn in locks and heavy objects to pick up. I attacked the adult playcentre with gusto. I got full marks apart from a point dropped for struggling to pick out coins from a deep bag and half a point for 'adapting' the grip with my thumb when picking up a kettle.

The x-rays showed little obvious wrong with the joints in my finger although the tendons disappeared at a funny angle. The manual dexterity test was more conclusive for the professional crowd of the registrar, the plastic surgeon and the occupational therapist, all together with Mary and me for the final make-your-mind-up session. There were too many potential negatives to surgery and the dexterity test showed that the hand was really already very good and almost certainly as good as it was likely to get.

So I'm resolved now that my left hand is the right hand, in the sense that whichever hand I choose to do something with is the right hand to do it with. And, like the revising for exams, I'll just have to practise to improve my toss at tennis.

THE FUTURE

I'VE STOPPED WRITING about my past at this point. In the meandering, one-legged walk-through of my life I've reached my mid-twenties; I'm about to meet my first wife, Jane, settle down and have children. I showed my early mentor Hugh Black-Hawkins what I'd written so far of this memoir. He said: "This book is about you growing up, dealing with your disability and sorting out your sexuality. The moment of marriage is the moment this drama ends. The search is over; it's a natural end for the book." The second 25 years will have to be in Volume Two.

What does the future hold in store for me? My mother and I met a man in Roehampton when I was a teenager. He was an ex-wicketkeeper and foresaw nothing but arthritis, pain and sorrow, as afflicted his cricketing fingers, for all the over-worked other, compensating parts of his and my body. It rattled me at the time – and I remember the incident clearly thirty five years on – but my mother and Jack Cosnett played down his negativity and advised me to carry on, to wait and see and to think positive.

Like all my friends and opponents at the tennis club my body has suffered 'wear and tear'. My left knee is slightly suspect at certain angles – a Chelsea player would probably have had keyhole surgery on it by now. My back spasms occasionally – picking up a bunch of leaflets from a bottom drawer of a Camden library filing cabinet; wrenching the steering wheel into full lock trying to get the truck out of Maiden Lane; picking up toddler son Matthew when sitting too far away. A few years ago a chiropractor gave my pelvic girdle full marks for level pegging and cleared the artificial leg of any backache blame, which is a tribute to generations of leg fitters over the years. Ironically human error, when fitting my latest new technology foot, led to me pounding around for a month on a leg that was a full two inches too long. Yes, of course it felt odd to wear, but I was assured that the new springiness of the new, even more dynamic foot could impact right up the leg. I still think the physiotherapist shouldn't have told me that maybe my walking style had been wrong all these years and I should try to change where I place my foot when I walk. When I was starting to get backache and a sore hip I took it to another chiropractor who quickly diagnosed the different length legs as the obvious problem. Nothing that a hacksaw couldn't quickly solve. The danger for me though is serious damage that will speed up my loss of mobility.

Because I am older any wounds or abrasions do take longer to heal, so I must take good care of the fleshy part and trust the fitters and mechanics to take care of the rest. Suddenly 'having another one in the car' is particularly attractive as an instant fix for a dodgy leg. If only it was so simple for other parts of the body.

It was a sense of the onset of the odd creak and tweak of age that led me to consult my doctor about my right hand. But, as explained above, the advice I got was that the hand was pretty good and that an operation was just as likely to make things worse than better. Back to squeezing the tennis ball and hoping the left hand holds up and the same for my dependency on my left, hopping, leg.

Without a clear explanation of the causes of my missing fingers and toes, I had no way of knowing for sure if this would pass on to my children. Of course we would love them unconditionally but, until society switches to counting in Base 8, ten fingers are an asset for the decimal world. I remember feeling that I did not want them to have any disadvantage – although the distinct disadvantages in my life from my disabilities are very few.

I was pretty tense when we saw the scan of my first child, Matthew. It was quite an emotional moment of relief to count the full set of digits as he (eventually) came out. Matthew's head got stuck on the way out – big head like his dad. The medical staff decided to apply the Foetal Scalp Monitor to keep an ear on the heart rate in case of distress. As they stuck the hook into Matthew's head, and removed the belt monitor, the heartbeat display on the machine flat-lined alarmingly. Never mind the baby, the parents' distress levels were soaring. Then a midwife muttered: "Doctor, the FSM is plugged out..." i.e. they had forgotten to plug the bloody thing in. Soon the reassuring sound of heartbeat/galloping horses resumed, until a large pair of tongs pulled the boy out. Second child, Robert, scored a very high (1 in 13 chance) score on the prediction for Downs Syndrome or other possible concerns. Could this be related to my genetic legacy? But he popped out like a perfect pumpkin and has developed into the sort of sports-mad athlete that I wonder sometimes if I might have been. His sister Katherine is much the same, perhaps even sportier, only more sensible...

There will be a faint holding of breath for me when, or if, Matthew, Robert or Katherine have any children. I hope to become a wicked granddad. I want to scandalise the grandchildren by touching things in shops and foreign airports that say "Do not touch" and complaining to the staff about food or service in restaurants. I want to play "This is the way the farmers ride" with them without my leg falling off before the bit about the huntsmen falling into the ditch. I want to play on the beach with them and for them not to mind if people keep staring at my legs in my unfashionable shorts.

But most of all I want my unknown legacy (with an emphasis on the 'leg') to remain with me and not to reappear down the generations. I want my 'unique selling point' to remain unique to me. Although, if one of the grandchildren inherits my artificial leg signed by Glenn Hoddle, I hope they get a good price for it on E-bay

In France with Mary, Katherine, Matthew and Robert, 2008

2043. The small invalid trike with yellow wheels hurtled down the steep hill. The old man's feet were no longer on the pedals controlling the front wheel. The man's granddaughter began to run but she was too far behind to reach him. The trike reached terminal velocity and the junction at the bottom of the hill loomed. The old boy heard his granddaughter cry out with increasing anxiety – much to his satisfaction. As he whizzed past the last house but one, he jammed his metal leg under the wheels and they froze. The trike slewed to a halt leaving a very pleasing skid mark down a series of paving stones. He turned and grinned at his granddaughter who was just arriving out of breath: "That was fun! Can we do it again?" "Perhaps tomorrow", she winced.

ERIC THE RABBIT

I WILL TELL YOU a tale about Eric the Rabbit,
Who was given the chance, and elected to grab it,
Of going to Paris, or else to Madrid,
With expenses all paid and with two hundred quid.
You might ask: "How did Eric, a shy sort of chap,
Engineer this arrival in luxury's lap?"
And the question's a good one, and one much repeated
By the guard on the train whereon Eric was seated
And also the pilot who 'flew him the flag'
And also the porter who carried his bag.
For it did not occur to them all in the slightest
That, of bunnies they'd met, Eric quite was the brightest.
The answer is: though he did everything well,
It was crosswords where Eric could really excel.
The discovery of young Eric's masterly touch
Was made when The Times went to lining his hutch.
The next morning, though much was just fit for the bin,
The crossword was pristine and properly filled in.
Once the crossword bug bit Eric soon was a guzzler
Til one day they bought him a copy of Puzzler,
And the fiendishly hard competition he did
Gave the winner a choice of 'Paree' or Madrid
I am sure that I hardly need tell you all that
Eric Rabbit's the name they pulled out of the hat
(True poetic justice for the ranks of the hoppers
Some of whom spend their lives being dragged out of toppers!)
It was so, fluffy Eric had actually won
And I'll tell you all now of his trip to the sun.
To the man from The Puzzler the shock was quite horrid
And brought beads of cold sweat to his puckered-up forehead,
And, though drenched, could do nothing but sit there and dab it
And think how to deal with a VIP rabbit.

But there truly was little the fellow could do
To remove Eric's right to a sun-trip for two.
His choice of companion was total simplicity
As for months he'd admired a frog called Felicity,
Whose green skin and pink eyes more attractive he'd found
Than most others he'd met with the other way round.
She was thrilled by the invite and jumped at the chance
But was keen to dissuade Eric plumping for France,
For she'd heard of these foreigners' culinary habits
That were even unkinder to frogs than to rabbits.
And though Paris is where many people prefer,
In Madrid she might keep both her legs where they were.
And so Eric, as faithful to her as a dog,
Chose Iberia, just to placate his fair frog.
So the Puzzler Man, driven half-way insane,
Booked a rabbit and frog on the plane bound for Spain.
And, though previous to this he had not been a worrier,
Was perturbed by the prospect of acting as courier,
For though widely experienced before in this post
He knew nothing of what rabbits liked to do most.
In the meantime the couple were raring to go
And they hopped on the Tube that went out to Heathrow.
British Airways did well with an improvised lunch
Of 'squashed fly' biscuits and lettuce to munch,
But the free Dry Fly sherry did more than the food
To put Eric quite firmly in 'holiday mood'
And Felicity, brought up on juices of fruit,
Found the gin heavy going and was 'tired' (as a newt).
To the man from The Puzzler this whisky galore
To his balance of mind was the vital last straw.
He made up his mind, touching down at Madrid,
Of Felicity and Eric he would have to be rid.

He vowed there and then they would never get far back,
As he helped the drunk bunny tumble onto the tarmac.
In the course of the following day his duplicity
Ensnared hapless Eric and fair-faced Felicity.
In the morning, Ol' Bright Eyes was frankly more foggy
As he blearily peered at his quite groggy froggy,
And he croaked his replies even better than she did,
When the Puzzler Man said he knew "Just what was needed":
A bullfight was on in the centre of town
Where neither need speak and where both could sit down.
And Eric just nodded, not risking a sound,
Being pleased to avoid too much hopping around.
When they got to the bullring they found it was full
Of fools watching others being chased by a bull.
Soon the couple recovered enough to applaud
And shout out: "Ole!" every time one was gored.
At a gap in the action, the Puzzler Man said
He'd arranged Eric's meeting the man in the red
(With a cloak of a similar colour) as guest,
and that: "This was the way" and he "Wished him the best".
So they took Eric down and they planted him at a door
And then ushered him through face to face with the matador.
He thought it all rather a singular thing
They should both be there standing alone in the ring,
But the man seemed friendly enough kind of chap,
Who held Eric up for the people to clap,
And Eric was stunned at the fame one may gain
Just from filling crosswords and flying to Spain...
But the very next moment, he was stunned even more
When the Spaniard let go and he fell to the floor,
And thus didn't pinpoint the Puzzler Man's smirk
As he flogged "a fat frog" to a man from Dunkerque.

The matador, faced with a powerless rabbit,
Attempted to press his advantage and stab it,
With streamers that sported the colours of Spain,
And all the crowd bellowed "Ole!" yet again...
When our frog hit the bullfighter full in the face
And gave Eric Rabbit a moment of grace.
Just in time Eric woke to this turn of affairs
And they fled – to leave only a handful of hairs.
Now a trophy hangs over this matador's fire.
And THAT is the tale of E. Rabbit Esquire.

Eric the Rabbit troupe on tour
Back row L to R: Sue Vercoe (narrator), Sarah Chittenden (flute),
Veronica 'Bonk' May (oboe), Andy Feist (horn), HW (bullfighter),
Teresa Butler (clarinet),Graham Bull (composer/conductor),
Helen Williams (bassoon)
Front row L to R: Jane Heron (Felicity the Frog), Bob Hyman (Puzzlerman),
Bill Benson (Eric the Rabbit)